WHEN I AM LITTLE AGAIN

and

THE CHILD'S RIGHT TO RESPECT

by

Janusz Korczak

*Translated from the Polish
with Introduction by*
E.P. Kulawiec

Foreword by
Valerie Phillips Parsegian

Illustrations by
Gizela Gawronski

UNIVERSITY
PRESS OF
AMERICA

Lanham • New York • London

Copyright © 1992 by
University Press of America®, Inc.
4501 Forbes Boulevard, Suite 200
Lanham, Maryland 20706

3 Henrietta Street
London WC2E 8LU England

All rights reserved
Printed in the United States of America
British Cataloging in Publication Information Available

Original Titles:
Kiedy Znów Bede Maly (1925)
Prawo Dzlecka do Szacunku (1929)

Library of Congress Cataloging-in-Publication Data

Korczak, Janusz, 1878-1942.
[Kiedy znów bede maly. English]
When I am little again ; and, The child's right to respect /
by Janusz Korczak ; translated from the Polish with introduction
by E.P. Kulawiec ; foreword by Valerie Phillips Parsegian ;
illustrations by Gizela Gawronski.
p.   cm.
Translation of: Kiedy znów bede maly and
Prawo dziecka do szacunku.
1. Korczak, Janusz, 1878-1942—Biography—Youth.
2. Authors, Polish—20th century—Biography.
3. Educators—Poland—Biography.   4. Child rearing.
I. Gawronski, Gizela.   II. Korczak, Janusz, 1878-1942. Prawo
dziecka do szacunku.   English. 1991.   III. Title.   IV. Title:
When I am little again.   V. Title: Child's right to respect.
PG7158.G662A24   1991
891.8'58709—dc20   [B]   91-3759 CIP

ISBN 0–8191–8306–7 (cloth : alk. paper)
ISBN 0–8191–8307–5 (pbk. : alk. paper)

 The paper used in this publication meets the minimum requirements of
American National Standard for Information Sciences—Permanence
of Paper for Printed Library Materials, ANSI Z39.48–1984.

For Gretchie

Acknowledgements

That these translations might reach a larger audience is due to the encouragement of a number of people: Zbigniew Banaszak, Claire Walker, Marcus Ampadu, Eugene Slotkowski, Sam Kavruck, Kurt Bomze, Hilda Gruskin, and the members of the International Janusz Korczak Association. Mine is a modest but heart-felt expression of gratitude for their support.

Separate grants from the Joseph B. Slotkowski Publication Fund administered by the trustees of the Kosciuszko Foundation of New York and from Gretchen and Dan Gentile of Cleveland gave much needed material support as well for which sincere thanks is given.

E.P.K.

Contents

Introduction

One early August day in 1942 a bearded, old man was observed leaving the Warsaw Ghetto at the head of a long procession of children ranging in age from ten to eleven years. In neat rows of four, fifty rows in all, the children moved in an orderly manner through the hot summer streets of Warsaw toward the Umschlagplatz set up by the then-occupying German troops beside the Gdansk railway station not far from the center of the city. The old man at the head of the line, holding a child by each hand, walked with resolute step, in spite of a small frame weakened by fatigue and under-nourishment, giving courage and support to all those who followed behind. All eyes were upon the old man, a bright and hopeful beacon holding fast in a raging sea. The Warsaw Ghetto was being liquidated according to a master plan drawn up in the Berlin headquarter, and it was now the turn of the so-called "Little Ghetto", the children's institutions, of which the old man's orphanage was a part. When the procession reached the railway station, the children, the old man, and his co-workers were all loaded into waiting freight trains which, upon signal and with tightly locked doors, transported them eastward to the little village of Treblinka. And once out of the Warsaw station all trace of this human consignment vanished. In all likelihood the final destination was the extermination camp in the outskirts of the village.

This is the usual way in which most writing about Janusz Korczak, the old man who headed the procession, begins, contrary to the laws of life. His was a final and logical act in a lifetime devoted to the care and upbringing of children—other people's children. It was an act of choice and preference, an act of love and compassion in a world which had seemingly lost both. Although it was beyond his power to save his orphans from the Nazi plan, Korczak tried even in those final and hopeless days to make his children's "last outing" easier. It was his choice not to abandon them.

The old man, known universally by his pen name, Janusz Korczak, dedicated his life to the cause of the child's well-being as a medical doctor, educator, writer, lecturer, publicist, and radio commentator. He was a philosopher who stood beyond any official doctrine, a poet rooted in the culture and language of his native Poland, a scientist whose concern for the world and man verged on saintliness. Already in his sixties when the Germans occupied Poland in 1939, Janusz Korczak continued what had been his life-time work—this time directing his orphanage in the most trying of conditions within the Ghetto walls to which his children had been removed, choosing to remain with them in their re-location. The general recognition and esteem achieved by Korczak through his writings and his work made a different choice understandable. For Korczak, however, these were not considerations. He stayed with his children. And for the next two years in the Warsaw Ghetto he carried on what had been his life-long task as mentor, doctor, feeder, friend, and moral leader to some two hundred homeless Jewish orphans. In a diary which he kept during those days and which survived the war Korczak noted: "I have been watering the flowers, poor orphanage plants, Jewish orphanage plants. A guard stood outside and watched me as I worked. I wonder, does that peaceful work of mine at six o'clock in the morning annoy or move him?" Korczak must have had super-human strength and courage to carry on his work in a setting that resembled hell. "The surroundings change from day to day," he recorded elsewhere in his diary. "A prison, a plagued spot. A lunatic asylum, a gambling casino. Monaco. The stakes? One's head!"

Korczak's work in these last two years of his life have, in the course of time, taken on more and more the trappings of a legend, however correct the facts. His presence among the children and his co-workers gave the kind of support which was needed to carry on with some semblance of order. It also gave the needed illusion of an unbroken life pattern. With the close specter of death hanging all about life went on: school life continued, the children's organizations continued, the school newspaper, the daily chores, the recording and collecting of data—all part of Korczak's "system"—all went on as of old. It was only in his diary that Korczak expressed the mental and spiritual anguish which besieged him at this time. Without his presence the orphanage, the children, could not have held together as they did. Indeed, the orphanage, Korczak's orphanage, was an oasis in a barren desert thanks largely to him.

In one of his diary notations Korczak wrote: "I exist not to be loved and admired, but to love and serve. It is not the duty of those around me to love me. Rather, it is my duty to be concerned about the world, about man." And more poignant becomes the legend of Janusz Korczak, an elderly Pied Piper of our era, when one learns that he turned down repeatedly all offers of rescue by his friends to get him out of the Ghetto, to hide him in the country, to save him with forged documents and a safe place. But since these offers could not under the circumstances include his children as well, Korczak elected to remain with them to the final end, fulfilling his chosen commitment and duty toward his fellow man, his service. Choosing to serve for this man meant total commitment, complete dedication, an unswerving path. In Korczak the child had his best friend, his fiercest champion.

He was born Henryk Goldszmit in Warsaw, in 1878, into a middle-class Jewish family with a long history of assimilation into Polish culture. His father was a highly successful lawyer noted for his writings on law. His grandfather was a doctor, while his great-grandfather, a glazier. His early life was a care-free, protected, and happy one. A loving grandmother was a early influence. She took an active interest in him, paid attention to his early childhood interests and musings, sided with him on issues, and gave him a sense of assurance of his worth. This happy childhood, however, was abruptly shattered when he was eleven, by the death of his father, a tragedy which not only robbed the boy of a loving parent, but left the family without the means of support. The next few years were hard times indeed. Forced to move from spacious, elegant quarters to poor ones, the family had to scrape by on the barest of means. During his teen years, Korczak became the sole bread winner for his mother, grandmother, and sister by giving private lessons in after-school hours. At the same time, Korczak took a job as a volunteer in a neighborhood lending library. This was his first real brush with abject poverty, as he came in direct contact with the residents of the district serviced by the library. As a volunteer, Korczak organized a free reading club in the neighborhood and often conducted reading sessions in some of the living quarters of the library users. It was in a notorious slum district of the city and conditions in the rooms which Korczak visited reflected the impoverished state that prevailed. This early experience with the poor left a deep impression on the sensitive youth and, doubtless, was instrumental in his own choice of a career later on. As a writer he used his first-hand experience in his first novel, *Children Of The Street* (1901), a treatment of sociology in literary form. And later, as a doctor, Korczak gave up a lucrative practice among the rich to minister to the needs of the poor, both as a resident physician in a children's hospital and then later as an orphanage director.

Torn between writing and medicine as a career, Korczak chose the latter justifying his choice by saying: "Writing is only words. Medicine is deeds." As it turned out Korczak successfully merged both activities. Not only did he become a doctor-pediatrician but a writer as well uniting the scientific skills of research with the richness and sensitivity of descriptive prose. The combination was a fortuitous one. He acknowledged his debt to medicine in this way: "Medicine gave me the discipline of scientific thinking. Thanks to it I learned to relate diverse and scattered detail and contradictory evidence in a logical way."

Early on Korczak made a pronounced effort to incorporate his experience with children as a tutor and a doctor, to merge his experiences into a unified goal. In one of his first writings in the field of education he formulated his concept of what a school should be: "a forge where the most sacred slogans are stamped out, where everything which gives life should flow through it, which should issue the loudest call for the rights of man and which should most boldly and relentlessly condemn that which had become muddied in man." To serve the child then was his path to serve man.

Sensing the need to extend his range of knowledge, Korczak spent time abroad in Berlin, Paris, and London, studying the latest methods and approaches in pediatric medicine, his specialization. A much earlier trip to Zurich while still a university student in 1901, brought him a closer look at Pestalozzi's educational principles and practices with which he was fascinated since youth. Pestalozzi, as it turned out, was one of Korczak's favorite models, one where the child was the center-point of schooling, the focus. Korczak's own educational writings bear frequent references to Pestalozzi, while his own 'school' later bore a striking resemblance to Pestalozzi's philosophy. "We will build a school," wrote Korczak, "where children will not be learning dead letters from a life-less page; where, rather, they will learn how people live, why they live, how they can live differently, what they need to learn and do in order to live full of the free spirit."

While in London, visiting an orphanage in 1911, Korczak settled once and for all on his chosen path, one which he was to pursue for the remainder of his life. "For a son I chose the idea of serving the child and his rights," he acknowledged in a letter to a friend. Thus, in a single stroke, Korczak gave up the idea of marriage and a family, along with the prospect of a lucrative medical practice, and settled for a career in the service of children.

Ample opportunity and experience came his way in the ensuing years to support and sustain the decision he had made. In WW I Korczak was assigned to a children's home in Kiev while serving in the military as a doctor. Here he carried out extensive observations of pre-school and elementary school children. The materials he gathered from this experience resulted in a later book, *Educational Moments* (1919), in which he expressed the need for a close and critical observation of children free of any kind of subjectivity—the cornerstone of Korczak's scientific approach. Close and detailed scrutiny was the slogan of this tireless quest to learn and know the child. The volumes of recordings and observations began to mount, compilations of child growth and behavior, of children alone and children in groups, of children at work and children at play. He studied children at every possible moment and in every possible situation. He spent summers in vacation camps for Polish and Jewish children and studied children there as well, surrounded by and reacting with nature, freed from the constraints and squalor of their urban slums.

Two touching books resulted from this experience, one about Jewish children, *Moshki, Joshki and Srule* (1910) and another about Polish children, their counterparts, *Jozki, Janki, and*

Franki (Joeys, Johnnies, and Frankies) (1911). The contents of these two books, filled with episodes and stories about the young vacationers' activities, revealed what importance Korczak placed on detail, on some apparently insignificant happening, some trifle, always a clue for him to some larger meaning. "Here," Korczak revealed, "I met for the first time a group of children and in independent work learned the ABCs of educational practice. Rich in illusions and experiences, sentimental and young, I thought I could accomplish a great deal because I tried so hard."

The year 1912 was an eventful one for Korczak. He accepted the position of director of the Jewish orphanage in Warsaw called, "Dom Sierot" (Home of Orphans). His association with it lasted until the end of his life. Here Korczak was able to try out his "method" of up-bringing that, for its time, was unique, if not revolutionary. Impressed with Pestalozzi, fired by the entomologist Fabre, moved by Rousseau and Key, imbued with his own insights and impressions of child growth and development, Korczak dreamed of a school that recognized and gave vent to each child's right to respect. His orphanage became a democracy of children wherein children had a voice in governance, had duties and responsibilities, monitored their own work and progress, participated in daily routines of looking after property, organized their recreation, and developed social consciousness by peer cooperation and supervision. The orphanage had a constitution that empowered the children as the prime movers and doers of life in the orphanage. The adults there—Korczak and a handful of assistants—all came under the regulations described in its codex. The constitution provided for a children's court, a parliament, a court of peers, for a children's newsletter and a committee of guardians that would select child guardians for those children who needed one. It decreed that all children should have the right to be loved, the right to be listened to, the right to respect, the right to a past and a present as well as a future. To prepare for life, Korczak tried to make life as real as possible in his orphanage. In his major work, *How To Love A Child* (1919) he mused: "For years I have been observing the quiet sadness of sensitive children and the brazen antics of grown-ups. The child has a right to be himself, has a right to respect. Before you make revolutions, before you make wars, think first of these proletarians with short legs, think first of the child." No starry-eyed romantic, Korczak, while giving children the opportunity to manage their own lives and to develop their natures as freely as possible, reserved the right as arbiter and overseer in this republic of children, recognizing the need for adult experience and wisdom, adult intervention lest his republic become a free-for-all. If the success of this approach was to be measured by the kind of cooperation and group cohesion that was promoted, then Korczak's democracy, from all accounts, succeeded.

If the child's welfare was Korczak's first passion, then writing had to be a close second. Since his earliest written piece, a play, entitled *Which Way?* (1899), which was awarded a first prize in a national competition, Korczak wrote and published continuously till the end of his life. Apart from purely medical subjects, he dealt primarily with the subjects of children, social behavior, education, and child up-bringing. He attached special attention to the latter which was in keeping with his idea of reforming the world, making the world a better place. And his medium for this transformation he believed was the child. "To reform the world," he noted, "means to reform the method of bringing up children." This thought found full voice in his now classic novel *King Matt The First* (1923). In it Korczak's reformer is none other than a boy-king, Matt, who struggles unsuccessfully to bring about a world reformation, one based on mutual trust and cooperation between children and adults. This same theme, the child's position in a world ruled by adults, is reflected in other books, notably *Fame* (1913); *When I Am Little Again* (1925); and *Rules For Living* (1930).

Finally, mention needs to be made of one of Korczak's highly successful 'experiments' illustrating the trust and confidence he placed in children. In 1926, Korczak launched *The Little Review.* This was a weekly supplement to the Jewish daily, *Our Review*, published in Warsaw. The supplement was written entirely by young people for their own kind. Children and youth all over Poland served as correspondents gathering newsworthy stories of interest to children. This was possibly the first venture of its kind in the history of journalism. In his appeal Korczak wrote to his future readers at the launching that the magazine "will consider all problems of learners, and school, and it will be edited in such a way as to defend children." The only adult serving on the editorial board was Korczak himself at the beginning, and then later, when the publishing became a full-time task, his secretary, Igor Newerly. Otherwise the children were the principal workers. They all met once a week to discuss articles, issues, concerns, letters and inquiries sent from around the country. Korczak's role in this was that of guide and helper, otherwise the paper was truly the work of the children. Its success was nation-wide and lasted until the war broke out in 1939.

In all his work with children, Korczak strove to serve more as facilitator and guide, relying on the native and natural abilities of the young to carry the burden of action. He strove to instill in his charges the ideas that the responsibility for their actions lay with them, that placed in situations that challenged their behavior children would be able to cope, and that the best way to prepare children for life was to have them experience situations that were real. All his methods served this goal. Korczak, the adult, aware and wise of the adult world, tried to make best use of his knowledge in preparing his children to "enter the ranks" in a way that there would be few surprises and fewer shocks. Work with self-government, with the children's newspaper, work in the summer camps, all were used with this in mind. These attempts must be considered striking innovations in child-rearing practices in the early part of this century. Korczak together with other child advocates of his day like Ellen Key, William Preyer, or Enlantyne Webb, tried to raise the consciousness of adults as to the dependent condition of the child and the effects that dependency could produce. Two of Korczak's works especially, *King Matt* and *The Child's Right To Respect,* could be seen as literary treatments of the Geneva Declaration of 1923, the Declaration of the Child's Rights, a result of the active work of the child advocates at the time.

A greater champion of children would be hard to find. Thanks to his writing, a kind of oral stream of consciousness, a blend of poetry and studied insight gleaned from careful observation, the reader is alerted to a deeper appreciation and reflection of the child's nature described in the following:

> "The child is a hundred masks, a hundred roles of a
> skilled actor. Different ones for the mother, and
> different ones for the father, grandmother, or
> grandfather; different ones for the stern or
> sympathetic teacher; different ones in the kitchen

or among peers, for the rich one and the poor one, and different ones for every day and holiday clothes. Naive and cunning, well-behaved and self-willed, he knows how to conceal and hide and play a role so well as to deceive and take advantage of us. Regarding instincts, he lacks only one—or, rather, he possesses it, splintered as it may be like a nebula of erotic premonitions. Regarding feelings, he surpasses us by a force unskilled in restraint. Regarding the intellect, he is at least our equal, lacking only experience. This is why an adult is so frequently like a child, and a child like an adult. Finally, all other differences boil down to the fact that he is not a wage earner, and being so dependent he is forced to give in to our will."

And what in the light of such an assessment of the child was Korczak's advice to those working with children, to parents and teachers?

"Let us demand respect for those clear eyes and smooth temples, that young effort and trust... Respect, if not humility, toward the white, bright, and unquenchable holy childhood..."

When Janusz Korczak took the last march with his children to the train depot loading area and the open doors of the freight trains there in August, 1942, it was the final cap-stone expression of a life style, a philosophy that indelibly defined his notion of commitment—commitment to an idea that began as a teen-ager in a lending library in a poor Warsaw neighborhood, found voice on a trip to London as a young medical student, and was sustained for the remainder of his adult life as the director of orphanages, the idea that a better life for mankind began with the bettering of the up-bringing of children. "One's words," he wrote once in a letter to a friend, "have only so much value as one imparts to them by the action of one's own life." In words and deeds Korczak imparted such value, gave credence to all that he wrote and labored over in behalf of the child, was steadfast in his conviction. He gave his life.

E.P. Kulawiec
University of Southern Maine

Foreword

> "When I was big, the more interested I was in something, the better I could talk about it. But it's different with children. If something interests them very much, then that's the very reason it's difficult to describe it."

Janusz Korczak here expresses perfectly the conversational conundrum between children and ourselves. By the time a child can articulate his or her deep-felt thoughts he no longer is a child, and we have at once lost exact touch with our own past and with the inhabitants of our future.

Fortunately, two writers of this century have been able, by the grace of their literary art, to bring the living world of the child to light. In *À la recherche du temps perdu* (1918), Marcel Proust brought back, in vivid and lasting detail, the small feelings of childhood remembrance. But he did it with analytical elegance, so the reader always knows Proust is big recalling when he was little. Korczak's *When I Am Little Again* (1925) accomplishes something much more difficult. With Korczak you know he is little recalling when he was big. Both writers lift the scabs of time, but of the two Korczak is the more revealing and the more healing.

Korczak limns the searing humiliation of childhood through simple exchanges such as this one:

> "Once I asked, 'Mama, is a red ribbon better for a dog or a cat?' And Mama answered, 'You tore your pants again today.'"

But Korczak can also be lyrical:

> "When I was a grownup and I saw snow, I already

xix

anticipated the slush that would follow. I felt the damp overshoes, and wondered whether there would be enough coal for the winter. And joy—it was there, but sprinkled somehow with ashes, dusty and grey. But now I feel only that white, transparent and blinding joy. Why? For no reason at all: because it snowed!... There are thousands of little sparks inside me. It's as if someone sprinkled diamond dust in my soul and along the ground. The dust was sown and now diamond trees will spring up and a wondrous fairy tale will be born."

Anyone who is around children, talking with them, will re-experience the "thousands of little sparks" enlightening memory, but most of us cannot describe the sensation. We recognize Korczak's observation that "it's easy to speak if you only just want to say something, but when you want to very much, it's really hard."

The gulf is actually larger than reticence. Anthropologists have studied the phenomenon of age-bounded cultures. For example, 8-year-olds the world over know certain jokes, pavement games, circumlocutions which we all knew as 8-year-olds but have lost by the time we were twelve or so. The lore gets passed on from 8-year-old generations to generations, a whole discrete international subculture forgotten by every adult. Except for a few rare and treasured moments of communication when an especially generous youngster breaks out and conveys his true feelings to us, we adults are given the chance to enter the world of the child only through books like *When I Am Little Again*.

In describing M. Legrandin inveighing against snobs, in *Swann's Way*, Marcel Proust wrote: "He could not (from his own knowledge, at least) be aware that he was one also, since it is only with the passions of others that we are ever really familiar, and what we come to find out about our own can be no more than what other people have shown us. Upon ourselves they react but indirectly, through our imagination, which substitutes for our actual, primary motives other, secondary motives, less stark and therefore more decent." Korczak performs the miracle of translating the "passion of others" directly to the reader's imagination. Whether we take the experience straight or filtered through secondary motives, we at least have direct access to the feelings of our pupils, our children, our successors.

So be forewarned. The perfect anecdotes of Selma Fraiburg or Benjamin Spock, the careful descriptions of Jean Piaget or Maria Montessori, are here sustained and developed. Korczak knows where all the bruises are, and probes each one. He evokes those helpless moments when the child is arrayed against all adults because children are lumped as one in the adults' eyes. "The saddest thing is that one person can cause everyone so much unpleasantness and trouble... Your own criminals sit behind bars while ours walk freely among us."

> "I wanted to be little again to get rid of those grey adult cares and sorrows, but instead, I have those of a child, and they hurt even more... Don't let our laughter deceive you."

Don't let the power of Korczak's child-narrative deceive you either. For his complete narrative, and his life's message, is still that the child's laughter is full of hope along with the pain. This book puts us in touch with our own personal pasts, with the present of all the children we encounter, and thus with our collective future. Few books published today accomplish as much. This one is long overdue.

Valerie Phillips Parsegian

WHEN I AM LITTLE AGAIN

To The Adult Reader

You say:
—Dealings with children are tiresome.
You're right.
You say:
—Because we have to lower ourselves to their intellect.
Lower, stoop, bend, crouch down.
—You are mistaken.
It isn't that which is so tiring. But because we have to reach up to their feelings. Reach up, stretch, stand on our tip-toes.
As not to offend.

To The Young Reader

There are no exciting events in this story. This is an attempt at a psychological tale. No, not about the kind of psychology that was conducted on dogs. And not even about dogs, but only about one dog, Patch.

In Greek the word 'psyche' means soul. What is written here happens in the soul of man; what he thinks and feels.

This is how it was:

I'm lying in bed. I'm not sleeping. Only I'm recalling that when I was little. I often thought about what I would do when I grew up.

I imagined all sorts of things.

When I'll be big, I'll build my parents a house. And I'll have a garden—and I'll plant flowers too, in such a way that when one would fade others would bloom.

I'll buy some books too, with pictures in them or, better, without pictures, just so they're interesting.

And I'll buy paints, colored pencils, and I'll draw and paint. I'll draw whatever I happen to see.

I'll take care of the garden, and I'll build a summer house in it. And in the summer house I'll put a bench and an armchair. The summer house will be overgrown with wild grape and when Papa returns home from work, he can sit comfortably there in the shade. He'll put on his eyeglasses and read the newspaper.

And Mama will keep chickens. And there will be a pigeon roost high up on a pole to keep the cat or any other harmful animal from breaking in. And I'll have rabbits and a magpie too, and I'll teach it to talk.

I'll also have a pony and three dogs. At first, I want to have three dogs and another time four. I even knew what names I would call them. Or, I would think, let there be three dogs: one for each of us. Mine will be called Bekas, while Mama and Papa can call theirs however they like.

Mama will have a little house dog. But if she prefers a cat, then she can have a cat as well. The animals will get used to one another. They'll eat out of the same dish. The dog will wear a red ribbon and the cat, a blue one.

Once I even asked Mama: "Mama, is a red ribbon better for a dog or a cat?" And Mama answered: "You tore your pants again today." And when I asked Papa: "Does every old man have to have a bench under his feet when he is sitting?", he answered: "Every pupil should earn good grades and he shouldn't stand in the corner." Well, I left off asking questions after that. I tried to answer everything myself.

Maybe I'll have hunting dogs. I'll go hunting and afterwards I'll bring everything I catch home and give it to Mama. I'll even hunt some wild animal, but not alone, only with my friends. My friends will already be big too.

We'll go swimming. And we'll make a boat. If my parents want to, I'll give them a ride in it.

I'll have lots of pigeons too. I'll write letters and the pigeons will deliver them for me. These will be my carrier pigeons.

It was the same with cows. First I think that one will be enough, another time, two. And since we'll have cows, then we'll also have milk, butter and cheese. And the chickens will lay eggs.

Later there will be bee hives and we'll have bees and honey. Mama will make plum jam for our guests, enough to last the whole winter. And she'll prepare some marmalade too.

And there will be a forest nearby. I'll go to the forest and spend the whole day there. I'll take along enough things to last me a day and I'll go to gather berries, wild strawberries, and later, mushrooms. We'll dry the mushrooms and have them as well.

I'll cut lots of wood, for the whole winter, so that we'll be warm.

And a deep well has to be dug for water, right down to a clear spring.

But a lot of things will have to be bought too—shoes and clothing. Papa will already be old and he won't be able to earn much anymore. Therefore, I will have to. I'll hitch up the horse and take the fruits and vegetables to market; everything that has to be taken. And what will be needed at home, I'll bring. I'll drive a good bargain there and buy everything at a good price.

Or else, I'll put the apples in baskets and go off with them to distant lands by ship. In warm countries they have figs, dates and oranges, and people there get tired of them. And they'll want to buy my apples. And I will buy their fruits. I'll also bring home a parrot, a little monkey, and a canary.

I don't know myself whether I really believed in all this. But it was pleasant to imagine such things.

Sometimes I even knew if our horse would be a bay or a black. Because, for example, I see some horse somewhere and think: "Oh, I'll have such a horse when I grow up." And afterwards, I'll see a different one elsewhere and think: "No, this one will be better."Or else, "I'll have two then—this one and the other."

Then sometimes I'll dream something entirely different: that I'll be a teacher. I'll summon all the people together and tell them: "You must build a good school, one where it won't be cramped inside. Otherwise, the children will bump one another, and step on each others' toes, and push."

The children come to school and I ask them: "Guess what we're going to do?" One of them will answer: "We're going on a picnic." Another: "We're going to get slides." And this and that. And then I tell them: "No, no. We'll do all that too, but something even more important." And when they all quiet down, I add: "I'm going to build you a new school."

And I imagine all sorts of obstacles hindering me. That the school is almost finished when it suddenly collapses or else burns down. Then I have to start all over again. But, as if out of spite, I build even a better one.

I always thought by way of obstacles. If I'm travelling somewhere by ship, then there's a storm. If I'm in charge of something, some project, at first it doesn't go well, and it is only in the end that I succeed.

Because it is boring if everything goes well from the very start. And so, we have a skating rink beside the school, and all sorts of pictures, and maps, and stuffed animals, and a lot of equipment for the classes and for gymnastics.

The holidays are approaching and here the children have all gathered in front of the school and are shouting: "Please, Sir, we don't want a holiday; we want to go to school!" The janitor argues with them but it doesn't help. And I'm sitting in my office and don't know what is happening because I'm writing some papers... Until the janitor comes in. He knocks on the door first, and then enters: "Sir"... And then he tells me. "Excuse me, Sir, but the children have gone on strike. They don't want to take a vacation. "That's all right", I answer, "I'll calm them down right away."

I go out, laughing to myself. I'm not angry at all.

I explain to them: "A vacation's a vacation. Teachers have to rest. You know yourselves that when they're tired, they get angry and yell at you."

They heed my advice after a fashion. They're going to come to school, but only to the playground. They're going to play there and they'll keep order themselves.

I dreamed up a lot of different things I would do when I grew up. Once I thought that there would only be the three of us: Papa, Mama, and myself, while another time I thought that I would have a wife and be on my own.

It's a pity to separate from my parents and so, we all live together in the same house—only across the hall from each other. On one side of the house are my parents, and on the other side, my wife and I. Or else, I imagine two little houses, side by side. Because older people like quiet. When they take a nap after dinner, the children won't disturb them. Children, you know, run around, shout, jump; they yell and make a lot of noise.

I have a little bit of a problem with the children, because I don't know whether I want only boys or also a girl. And then, is it better for the boy to be older, or the girl?

My wife could be like my mother, and the children—I myself don't know. Do I want them to be aggressive or quiet? and what should they be allowed to do? Well, they shouldn't touch other people's things; they shouldn't smoke and use bad words; and they shouldn't fight or argue.

But what will I do if they really do fight, or if they won't want to obey or if they should cause some kind of trouble? Should they be taller than I or shorter?

I think up all sorts of things.

Once I want to be as big as Michael. Another time I want to be like Kostek or else like Papa. Then I think that I'd like to be so big forever, and again, only briefly, as a trial, because maybe at first it might be pleasant but then, afterwards, I'd want to be small again.

And I thought and thought until I really did become a grownup. I already have a watch and a moustache and a desk with drawers—everything, in short, that grownups have. And, the truth is, I really am a schoolteacher.

I'm not happy though. No, I'm not happy. The children don't pay attention in school, and I'm always angry. I have lots of worries. Neither my father nor mother are alive anymore.

Well, all right then: Now I'll begin thinking just the opposite.

"What would I do if I were little again?" Not so small, but big enough to be going to school again, to be playing with my friends again. If only to wake up suddenly and discover: "What's happened? Am I only dreaming, or is it real?" I look at my hands and I'm surprised. I look at my clothes and I'm surprised still more. I jump out of bed and run to the mirror. "What's happened?"

And here, Mama is asking: "Did you get up already? Hurry up and dress then or else you'll be late for school."

If I were a boy again, I'd want to remember and know everything that I know now. Only I wouldn't want anyone to find out that I was already a grownup once. I would pretend as if nothing were the matter; that I'm the same kind of little boy as all the others; that I have a mother and father and that I go to school. It would be really exciting this way. I would just observe everything and it would be very amusing that no one can recognize me.

As so, I'm lying in bed—I'm not sleeping. I'm day-dreaming.

"If I knew then, I'd never want to grow up. It's a hundred times better to be little. Grownups are unhappy. It isn't at all so that grownups can do whatever they want to. We have even less freedom than do children. And our cares and responsibilities are heavier. We have more sorrows too. And we have happy thoughts less frequently than do children. We don't cry anymore, that's true, but probably because it isn't worth crying. We only sigh deeply."

And here I sighed.

I sighed deeply. It's too bad; it's finished with.

No one can help now. I'll never be a child again. Feeling sorry won't help.

And when I sighed, it suddenly became very dark in my room. I can't see anything. Only there's a kind of smoke hanging in the air. My nose pinches too. And then the door creaked suddenly, and I got frightened. And all at once a tiny light appeared in my room, like a little star.

"Who is it?"

And the little star glides through the darkness, closer and closer toward me. It's already by my bed, and then suddenly it's on my pillow.

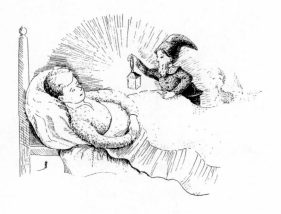

I look, and it's a little lantern. And on my pillow there is standing a tiny, little man. He has a white beard and on his head there is a high red hat. So-o-o-o, it's an elf. Only he's so tiny—like my little finger.

"Well, here I am."

He is smiling and waiting.

And I smiled too. Because I thought that I'm dreaming. Grownups too sometimes have children's dreams.

And the little elf says: "You called me, so I came. What do you want? Only you have to be quick about it."

He doesn't talk, but rather chirps, only softly. And I hear everything and understand.

"You called me", he says, "and now you don't believe."

And he began to swing his lantern, right, left, right, left...

"You don't believe", he says. "In olden times people believed in magic. Nowadays, only children believe in magicians, and fairy godmothers, and tiny elves."

He swings his lantern and nods his head. I'm afraid even to move.

"Tell me what your wish is. What is it you want from me? Try. What's the harm in it?"

I moved my lips to ask him, but he already guessed, he already knew.

"You called me with the Sigh of Longing. People think that it's a magic spell, that there have to be special words. But no, no. Not at all."

He nods his head no, and shifts his body from one leg to the other. It looks so funny as he does it. And his lantern is swinging from right to left. And I feel that I'm already falling asleep. But I open my eyes wide in order to keep awake. I would be sorry afterwards.

"Well, look now", says the tiny elf, "look how stubborn you are. Hurry up now, or I'll go. I can't stay long. And then you'll be sorry."

I even want to say something, a word, a greeting, but I can't.

Maybe that's how it is in real life: it's easy to speak if you only just want to say something, but when you want too very much, it's really hard.

I notice that the elf looks worried, concerned. And I feel sorry for him. But I can't utter even a single word.

"Well, you can relax now. Only it's a pity."

And he starts to leave. And it is only now, at this very moment that I utter something, quietly and quickly.

"I want to be little again."

He turned back and he swung around in such a way that his little lantern shone straight into my eyes, blinding me. He said something too, but I didn't hear. Nor do I know how he left either. But when I awoke in the morning, I remembered everything exactly.

I inspect my room carefully.

No, no. I wasn't dreaming at all.

It really happened.

The First Day

I don't tell anyone anything, that I was a grownup once. I pretend that I was always a little boy and I wait to see what will come of this. It seems so strange and funny to me. I observe everything around me and wait.

I wait until Mama cuts me a slice of bread, acting as if I can't myself. Mama asks if I did my lessons. I say that I did but, in truth, I really don't know.

Everything is as if in the fairy tale about the sleeping beauty, only maybe even worse. Because the princess slept a hundred years and everyone else slept at the same time and when they awoke they all awoke together; even the cooks and the flies awoke at the same time—the whole retinue, and the fire in the oven which was asleep too. And they all awoke just as they were when they fell asleep too. While I, on the other hand, awoke completely transformed. I looked at the clock, but immediately turned my eyes from it so as not to give myself away. Maybe that other boy didn't know how to tell time.

I wonder about school, how it will be there and what kind of friends I'll meet. Will they notice anything? Will they guess that I've attended school for a long time already? It's strange that I know to which school I have to go, on what street. I even know that my class is on the first floor and that I sit in the fourth seat near the window. And that beside me sits Gajewski.

I walk or, rather, march. I swing my arms. I feel light and rested: just the opposite from when I was a teacher. I look around in all directions and bang a metal sign with my hand. I don't know why I did that. It's so cold that my breath freezes. I blow on purpose to make a cloud of vapor. I remember that I can whistle like a train, blow smoke, and run fast. But I seem to be

15

ashamed to do these things. But why, after all? That's why I wanted to be a child again, to be happy.

But you can't do everything all at once. You have to look at everything first, beforehand, and then maybe later...

There are some boys and girls walking to school and there are even some grownups on the street. I look to see who is happier. These are quiet and so are those. It's true though, they can't show off in the street. And also, they haven't had time to relax yet. But for me it's different; it's the first day that I begin to be a child again. And that's the reason I feel so happy.

And somehow, I feel strange too, as if I'm afraid of something.

But that's nothing. That's how it must be on the first day. Later, I'll get used to it.

Until I spotted a big wagon; and the horse can't seem to manage it. It must be that it was shod wrong, because its legs keep slipping. A couple of boys are standing near-by, looking on. And I come up to the horse too.

"Will it move or not?"

I rub my ears and stamp my feet which are freezing; I want the horse to move...I'd regret having to leave and not knowing how this would end. It's always interesting to watch, because maybe the horse will fall—and then, how will his driver manage? If I were big, I'd walk right by indifferently and probably wouldn't take any notice. But because I'm little, it interests me. I notice how the grownups push us from their way, because we're bothering them. Why are they always in such a hurry?

Well, nothing came of it. The wagon finally started moving and I arrive at school. I hang up my coat in the cupboard. And they're already saying that the Vistula froze over.

"Last night."

Someone says that it isn't true. There's an argument. They aren't really arguing, they're just bickering. One of them says: "Look at him, will you! The first frost and the river's frozen over. Maybe there's an ice floe too?"

"Of course there isn't!"

"Oh, you're all mixed up."

A couple of others joined in. A grownup would probably have said that they're arguing. And that may be right too. This one says "You're crazy", another, "Stupid." From the Vistula they passed on to snow. Will it snow or won't it? And someone says that if the smoke from a chimney goes straight up, there won't be any snow. Another says that you can tell by the sparrows if it will snow or not. Someone else says that he saw a barometer. And again:

"You're crazy."

"I suppose that makes you smart."

"You're lying."

"Maybe you are."

Not everyone takes part in the argument. Some just stand around and watch. I'm listening too, and I recall that grownups quarrel frequently in their cafes—not about snow, but about politics. Exactly in the same manner. They even talk the same way:

"I bet that the president won't resign."

And another: "I bet that it won't snow."

They don't say, "You're crazy," or "You're lying."—they argue more delicately, but noisily too.

And so, I'm standing there this way, musing, when Kowalski dashes in. "Listen, did you do the homework? Let me have it, will you? I'll copy it for myself. We had company yesterday. Maybe the teacher's going to check."

I don't say anything. I open my schoolbag and look inside. As if it weren't mine but that other boy's who was doing the homework for me.

In the meantime the bell rings. Kowalski doesn't wait for permission, but only grabs my pad and darts for his desk. And it occurs to me that if I copy it too, the teacher may discover it and will think that it was I who stole it. She'll even stick me in the corner.

It seemed funny to me to think that I might still stand in the corner. And Wisniewski asks: "What are you laughing at?"

"I remembered something", I say and continue laughing.

"Dope" he says. "He's laughing and he doesn't know why."

"Dope or not" I answer, "Maybe I know why I'm laughing, only I don't want to tell you."

"Some secret" he retorts, and walks away.

I'm surprised that I know all their names, seeing as it is the first time in my life that I'm laying eyes on them, and they on me. Exactly as if in a dream.

The teacher enters at this moment and Kowalski hasn't yet returned my pad. I call quietly to him: "Kowalski, Kowalski", but he doesn't hear or else, pretends that he doesn't. And the teacher says: "Why are you fidgeting there? Sit quietly."

I think: "Well, I've earned the teacher's first reprimand already."

I sit quietly because I don't have my pad. I hide behind the boy in front of me and wait to see what will happen. I'm a little afraid. And it isn't nice to be afraid either. If I were a grownup, I wouldn't be afraid. No one would copy exercises from me. But since I'm a pupil, and a friend asked me for them, I couldn't have refused. He would have said right off that I'm unfriendly and selfish. He would have called me a name and said that I wanted the teacher to praise only me and say that I wrote the exercises well.

I will probably be the best pupil in the class, because I already finished school once. I forgot some things, but there's a big difference between remembering something and learning everything all over again, anew.

The teacher is explaining grammar, but I know it already. She tells us to write and, here, I've written it in a flash. And I'm sitting. The teacher noticed that I'm not doing anything and asks me: "And why aren't you writing?"

"I finished already", I say.

"Then show me what you've written," she says, but in a way that sounded as if she lost her patience.

I don't like it either when I assign something for a whole hour and the pupils finish it sooner. Because when the teacher assigns work, he wants to relax until the bell; but they hurry and then get into trouble.

And so, I go up to the teacher and show her what I've done.

"Yes, it's good, but look, you've made one mistake."

"Where?" I ask, feigning surprise.

I made a mistake on purpose so that the teacher wouldn't find out that I already finished school once.

"Find it yourself", she says, "If you didn't hurry so, you could have written a perfect paper."

I return to my seat and pretend that I'm looking for the error. I pretend that I'm busy. I'll have to write my lessons more slowly, at least in the beginning. Later on, when I'm already the best pupil in class, the teachers will get used to my being so fast.

Well, and I'm already beginning to feel bored. But the teacher asks:

"Did you find your mistake?"

I answer that I did.

"Then show me."

"Yes," she says looking over my paper. And then the bell rings.

That's the signal for recess, when the bell rings. The janitor chases everyone out of the room, and throws open all the windows.

What will I do now? It seemed strange that I should run around with the other boys. -But I try like the others. It's pleasant and fun. Oh, how pleasant it is!

When I was a young man, I could run too, but only to catch a bus or at the train station. Sometimes, I played with my friend's children—I would make believe that I want to catch them and they would run away from me. But that was when I was a young man. Later on, I didn't even bother to run after the bus. What of it if I missed it? I'll wait for the next one. And if I chased after children in a game of some kind, it was only a few steps after which, I'd stamp my feet in place to frighten them. And they run and run and, only afterwards, from a distance they turn around and look. Or else, they'll run around me in a big circle while I pretend to dart after them. The child thinks that if I really wanted to catch him, I could, because I'm big. But I really couldn't. I'm strong enough, but my heart starts to beat fast, and I lose my breath. Yes, and I'd climb the stairs slowly, and even rest along the way if it happened to be very high up.

But now:

I run so hard that the wind beats against my face and screams. I'm covered with beads of sweat but that's nothing. It's so pleasing and gay. I even jumped from joy and shouted: "Oh-h-h it's great to be a boy!"

But I got frightened suddenly and looked around, to see if anyone overheard. He could think: "If he's so happy then maybe he wasn't always a boy."

I run so fast that everything darts past my eyes. I get tired, that's true, but it's enough to stop for only a brief moment, to catch my breath—and then, again, further. It's good it happened that I can run again and not—clop, clop, one step after the other.

Oh, you wonderful elf, how grateful I am to you!

Because for us, running is like a horse ride, a gallop, a race with the wind. You don't know anything; you don't think, nor do you remember anything; you don't even see—only you feel so alive, so full of excitement. You feel as if the wind were inside you and all around you. First, I'm the one who is chasing. Then it's me who's running away. It's all the same, who's running and who's chasing. Only faster! Faster! Then I stumbled and fell and banged my knee. It hurt. And then the bell again.

What a shame! If only it could have lasted a little while longer; just another minute.

Who's faster, you or I?

My leg doesn't hurt anymore. Again the wind beats against my eyes, my face. Again I rush headlong, without knowing or remembering; just to be first. By some miracle I overtake the other boys. I overcome the obstacles. There's the door—and grabbing hold of the railing, I bound upstairs. I don't look around, but I feel that they've all been left far behind. I win...I'm the first...I'm the fastest. And with all my strength, I rush down the narrow corridor and...Bang! right into the principal, so hard that he almost fell over.

It's true that I saw him, but I couldn't check myself in time. Just like a cabby or a truck driver. And at that moment I understood why children are blamed unjustly sometimes. An accident occurs or a mishap, but he's not to blame. Maybe I really fell out of practice. Has it been so many years?

I could have squeezed myself in among the others, because they all came running down the corridor now. But it's only the first day that I'm a pupil again, and so I stood there dazed and looking a little sheepish. I didn't even say "Excuse me." But the principal grabbed me by the collar and gave me such a shaking that I thought my head would come off. He's so angry that I can't even describe it.

"What's your name, you scamp?"

I'm terrified, my heart's pounding and I can't utter a single word. He knows that it wasn't on purpose that I ran into him; he should forgive me then.

Should I give him such a violent push again? But he could fall and get hurt. I want to say something, but I'm shaking all over and my tongue's tied in knots.

And the principal again gives me a sharp tug and yells:

"Are you going to tell me finally? I'm asking you, what's your name?"

And here, such a crowd has gathered around us. And they're all looking on. I'm ashamed before the crowd. But just at this moment my teacher comes by and chases them all to their rooms. I was left alone. I lowered my head like a criminal.

"Come to the office."

I say quietly: "Please, Sir, I'll be good."

"What are you going to start telling me now" he says. "When I asked you for your name, why didn't you answer?"

"I was ashamed. Everyone was standing around and looking."

"But you're not ashamed to run so hard, like someone gone mad? Come tomorrow and bring your mother."

I started to cry. Tears began to stream down my face, like peas. And my nose got stuffed up right away.

The principal looked at me. He seemed to take pity.

"Well, look here now" he begins, "it's not good to play so hard, because you only end up crying in the end."

If I apologize right at this moment, I see that the principal would forgive me. But I'm ashamed to apologize. And I feel like saying, "Punish me in some other way. Why should I worry my mother?"

But I can't. Tears interfere.

"Go to your class now. The lesson's begun."

I bow a little and begin to walk away. And everyone is again staring at me. And the teacher's looking too. Marylski nudges me in the back: "What happened?" I don't answer and he again asks: "What did he say to you?" I'm angry. Why is he bothering me? What business is it of his?

"Marylski, no talking, please.", the teacher comes to my rescue. Evidently, she wanted to leave me in peace too. She sees that I'm troubled and so, for a whole hour, she doesn't call on me to recite.

And so, I'm sitting and thinking. I have lots to think about. I'm not listening; I don't know what they're talking about. It just happens to be arithmetic. They go up to the blackboard, write and then erase. Then the teacher took a piece of chalk and is saying something, explaining something. I'm worse than deaf. Because I don't hear and I don't see either. And I don't even pretend that I know. The teacher could see at once that I'm not paying attention. She must be a good person, because another would have gone into a rage. Now I understand that when something goes badly for a child, then other things pile right on top of him, one after another. He suddenly loses confidence in himself. And it really ought to be that when someone is crying, another should praise, encourage, and console. But does a person really have to cry? Do I know? Maybe he does and maybe he doesn't.

And how did I behave when I was a teacher? In a lot of different ways. So it was—I ran right into the principal, and he at once grabbed me by the back of the neck. What else could he do? He got angry, but later he calmed down. Did he forgive me? He said: "Go to your class." That was all.

And I still don't know whether I should bring my mother or not tomorrow.

And I'm thinking to myself: "I'm only a child again for such a short time, and how much I've suffered already. I had a taste of fear twice: the first time when the boy took my pad—that was unpleasant; the second time—with the principal. And that didn't end yet either, because I myself don't know what to do."

I really swallowed a lot of shame when I was grabbed by the neck then like some criminal. It's certain that no one grabs a grownup like that, or shakes him when he bumps into someone accidently. It's true that grownups walk more carefully, but still, it happens sometimes. And children are even permitted to run. If it's allowed, then who should be more careful, I, a little boy, or the experienced teacher?

It's strange that I never used to think about this when I was big. I'm a child again barely a couple of hours, and already the first tears. It didn't last long, but I did cry. And even though my eyes are all dry now, I still feel hurt.

And that isn't all. I fell down too.

I lower my stocking and look; the skin on my knee is scraped—it's not bleeding, but it burns. It doesn't really hurt, but it aches sort of. At first I didn't feel anything, but now, when I'm sitting quietly and have problems...

It's barely two hours that I'm a pupil again, and already the teacher commented that I shouldn't fidget in my seat, that I should sit quietly. And what would have happened had she found out that I let someone copy my homework? What would happen if the teacher now told me, "Repeat."

I'm not paying attention; not at all. And in class not only do you have to sit quietly, but you have to listen too, and know what's going on.

I'm selfish and foolish and inattentive—all because I'm a child again. If that's the case, maybe it would have been better to remain a grownup.

And at this moment, I began to feel sorry for the horse which couldn't pull the wagon because it was badly shod, and the wagon was heavy and the horse's legs kept slipping on the ice. I thought for a second about the horse and then returned to my own thoughts. "Was it better when I was big? Maybe the principal will forgive me. Now I'll walk carefully along the corridor. Maybe it will really snow at night. And I miss the snow so much, like one's own brother."

At this very moment I was looking out the window. A big storm cloud slid over and covered the sun. I don't remember now whether they agreed finally that it would snow or not. I was thinking that in America grownup people also like to bet on everything.

Maybe children really aren't so different from adults, only they live differently, and have different rules. And outside, the cloud is getting bigger and bigger—and blacker. Then it occurred to me: "A child is like spring. Either it's nice and sunny and gay and pretty or else, suddenly there's a storm, lightening flashes, and then thunder. But a grownup is like a fog. A sad, grey fog surrounds him. He has neither real big joys, nor griefs. It's grey and serious. Because, of course, I remember myself, the way it was. Children's joy and sorrow gallop like the wind, while theirs only develop and unfold. I remember that too!"

I liked the comparison. Yes, if I had the choice to make it all over again, I'd still prefer to try it.

And in this way I grew calm and happy again. So calm that it was like going out into a field at night, where a light breeze gently brushes your face, as if someone were touching your cheeks with gentle hands. And there are stars in the sky. Everything is asleep... Only the smell of the field all about, and the woods nearby...

The hour flew by quickly. If I'm going to be a teacher again, I'll never bother a child who has a worry. I'll leave him alone to think; let him calm down and rest.

When the bell rang, I shivered all over.

And right away, they started to pester me: "Why were you crying? What did the principal say?"

Grownups say that you shouldn't fight. They think that you fight for fun. Indeed, there are those kind, bullies, who purposely look for fights with weaker boys. We avoid them, make way for them. But this only angers them the more. When our patience runs over though, then it's time for us to teach them a lesson. Fortunately, there aren't so many of them. They are our poison though, of course. And it's funny that grownups blame all of us alike, simply because of them. Grownups don't know what a real pest is like or a bully, someone who can drive even the gentlest person into a rage, to tears.

And so, I'm troubled. Of course, everyone can guess what the principal told me, if I practically knocked him down. Why should they ask then: "What", How?"

If it was only one person. But no. You manage to break away from one and another comes up to you—and then the whole episode again from the beginning. Can't they see that I don't feel like talking? I don't even know them; I hardly ever talk to them—and this one too: "So you ran into the principal. He probably told you to come with your mother."

They don't even let a person be sad. They'll nag after someone so long that his sadness turns into anger.

I answer the first one quietly; the second one impatiently, "Go away!", and the third, "Leave me alone."

The fourth one I push away.

Now Wisniewski comes up to me. He's already called me a sly one and a dope in the morning. And now he wants me to tell him everything. "Well, why are you crying? He really laced into you, didn't he? You should have said that they pushed you."

"If you want to, go and lie yourself", I say.

But I regretted this at once.

"Oh-h-h-h, what a truth teller we have here. Look boys, I've found a truth teller!" I want to go, but he holds me. "Wait up, why are you in such a hurry?"

24

He doesn't let me go; he walks beside me and pokes me with his elbow. Then I pushed him. But he persists even more. "Just you don't push that way again, because it isn't your school, see. He thinks that just because the teacher praised him for making only one mistake, he can go around knocking others down."

At first, I didn't notice what he was hinting at. Only now did I understand. I'm already at the door, but he still doesn't let me go.

"Little baby" he says, "Baby cried. The little girl cried." And he wants to stroke my face with his dirty hands. But I already raised my arm. He's strong, this Wisniewski. But I was so angry now that it was all the same to me: what will happen will happen. If a fight started, he would get it too. But I ask myself now: What would the principal say, if, by chance, he happened to walk by and see. Of course, I would be blamed. I had already gotten into trouble once before and now, again. Now he'll remember me. And if anything happens in the future, he'll be suspecting me immediately. Because I'm a trouble-maker. "I know you. This isn't the first time."

When I was a teacher, I used to say the same thing.

I'm lucky though, because just at this moment the teacher enters the classroom to see if everyone had left. "Go out boys. Go and play a bit."

And he, the shameless one, even complains to her: "Excuse me, Ma'am. I wanted to leave, but he won't let me."

I felt such a hatred toward him that I could spit.

"Well, allright. Go. Go now."

He closed one eye, twisted his mouth in a strange way and, like a clown, with wide steps, sauntered out of the room; and I after him. I don't go outside and only wait in the hall for the recess to end.

Mundek comes up to me. He glanced around and then said quietly: "Don't you want to go outside and play?"

"No", I answer.

He stood for a moment and waited to see if I wanted to talk with him. He's different. I tell him what happened.

"I don't know if he forgave me."

He thought for a second: "You have to find out. He spoke that way in anger. Go to his office. He probably forgot."

There was drawing too.

The teacher told us to draw something—anything we wanted to, a leaf, or a winter scene, anything. I take my pencil. What to draw now? I never learned how. When I was big, I didn't know how to draw either. In general, schools weren't very good in my time. It was strict and boring. They didn't allow anything. It was so cold and oppressive that, afterwards, when I dreamed about it, I awoke in a sweat and was always glad that it was only a dream and not real.

"You haven't begun yet?" she asks.

"I'm thinking how to begin."

The teacher has light hair and a happy smile. She looked me in the eye and said: "Well then, you think about it: maybe you'll think of something nice." And I don't even know myself why, but I said: "I'll draw a school as it was in the past."

"And how do you know how it was?"

"My father told me." Of course, I had to tell a lie.

"All right", she says, "that will be very interesting."

"Will it be good or not?" I think. "After all, children aren't such good artists." I draw clumsily, but that doesn't matter. At most, they'll only laugh. Let them. It doesn't really matter.

There are such paintings which are made up of three parts: one in the middle, and one on each side of this. Each part is different, but together, they form a whole. Such a picture is called a triptych.

I divided my paper into three parts. In the middle section I drew a school recess: how children run, or else, someone did something bad, because the teacher is pulling him by the ear and he's trying to pull loose and is crying. But the teacher is holding him firmly by the ear and with a kind of riding whip is hitting him on the back. The boy raised his leg in the air, and it looks almost as if he were suspended. The other children are looking on; their heads are bowed a little; they don't say anything because they're afraid.

That was in the middle.

On the right side I drew a classroom. A teacher is hitting someone's hand with a ruler. Only the teacher's pet in the first row is laughing—all the others in the class feel sorry.

And on the left side they're really using switches. A boy is lying on the desk and the janitor is holding his legs while the teacher of penmanship, with a beard, raised his hand with the switch in the air. It's such a gloomy picture—like in a prison. I used such dark colors. On top I wrote: "Triptych—An Old-fashioned School."

When I was eight years old, I went to such a school. That was my first school; it was called a preparatory school. I remember one boy who got the switch then. The writing teacher beat him. Only I don't know whether the teacher's name was Koch and the pupil's Nowacki, or whether the pupil was Koch and the teacher Nowacki.

I was terribly afraid then. It seemed to me that when they finished with him, they would take me next. I was ashamed too, because they beat you with your pants down. They unbuttoned everything—in front of the whole class.

Afterwards, I felt disgust at both the pupil and the teacher. And then, whenever anyone was angry or when someone yelled, I immediately froze and waited to see who was going to be punished. That Koch or Nowacki wasn't decent either. Once, when it was his turn to be the class monitor, instead of wetting the eraser under the pump, he went and peed on it and then bragged about it and told everyone. The teacher entered and asked that the blackboard be erased because it was dirty. No one volunteered to do it. He became very angry and took the eraser himself. And now I don't know if they began to laugh right then at that moment, or whether it was only after they told him. That's why the boy got the beating.

I was very small then, I remember. And that's when I started to go to school. But I see everything clearly as if it happened only yesterday. And I feel everything anew. I draw so hard that my pencil's racing about. I'm even surprised myself.

The heads of the children come out small, but I try to make each one different—in such a way that you could tell every grimace. Each figure is different; one boy is leaning, another is standing straight. I drew myself too, but not in the first row.

I'm drawing so hard that I feel my ears burning. I feel hot, as if I were racing. It's as if I were inspired. I already was a grownup, so that I know the word "inspiration." A famous poet wrote his Improvisations when he was inspired. And the prophets were inspired when they preached.

Inspiration—that's when a difficult task suddenly becomes easy. And it's especially pleasant to draw then, or to write, or even to cut out and make something. Everything seems to turn out well then, and you don't even know how it happens. It's as if someone were doing it for me and I were only watching. And when it's all finished, I'm surprised—as if it weren't my own work. I feel tired too, but pleased that it turned out so well. I feel inspired and I don't know at all what is happening around me. It seems to me that children often work under this spell, only others disturb them and interfere. For instance, you are relating something, or reading, or writing, and it turns out well. Or else, you understood the assignment immediately. Or else, you make a mistake, and maybe even not really a mistake, only it is very, very small, and here, they instantly interrupt and tell you to correct it, to repeat it, to add something; they explain. And all at once, everything is lost. You're annoyed and you don't feel like working anymore, and it doesn't turn out well.

Inspiration—it's like a conversation with God. And no one has the right to interfere then. You have to be alone so as not to know or hear anything around you. This is exactly how it was now. The teacher is standing behind me, looking at how I'm drawing and I take no notice of her and only go over my painting and make corrections here and there. I add only one little line, one dot, and each time it comes out better.

The teacher had to be standing there behind me for a long time, only I didn't know. I examined my drawing from a little distance and again add something, a line, more color, but each time more carefully. You can ruin it if you correct too much. And then I feel tired. Suddenly I sensed it. I raised my head and the teacher smiled and touched my cheek with her hand.

I don't like it when someone pets me or touches me. But now, the teacher's hand felt cool and soft. And I smiled.

"How do you know that it is called triptych?", she asks.

"I know. I saw it on a picture, a postcard, in church." I'm stammering, and I blush even more. But finally the teacher asks: "Can I?"

"Please", I say and hand her my pad. She examines some previous drawings first and then the last one. But Wisniewski jumped out of his seat, butting in and saying, "a triptych!"

I was afraid lest the teacher begin to show it around and praise it, saying that it's good. She should understand, of course, that a jealous person can always be found in such a group, or else, a clown who will afterwards make jokes and tease. The teacher, however, understood this because she told Wisniewski to go back to his seat and she told me simply: "Well, you rest now. You must be tired."

She closed my notebook and placed it carefully in front of me on my desk. Carefully and precisely.

I immediately had this thought that if I were to be a teacher again, I wouldn't throw the children's notebooks on the desks, nor would I make corrections on their papers with heavy marks, or in such a way that the ink would spatter all over. I would handle their notebooks as carefully and precisely as she did just now.

I rested quickly and then the lesson ended. And now I have to go to the principal's office. But the principal is standing in the doorway and so I held back. My teacher stopped too. I'm waiting on the side and I don't know what to say. And the janitor is coming up again.

"Excuse me, Sir" I began, and then repeated it, but I know that the principal doesn't hear because I said it so quietly. It's extremely unpleasant if you have to say something and you're ashamed to speak.

They are talking about their own affairs, but I don't know what it is. Nor do I hear. Then the principal turns to me: "Go to the sixth grade classroom and see if there is a globe there. Only fast, like lightening." And then he glanced at me and remembered, because he adds: "But don't run into anyone along the way."

I hurried at once to the sixth grade and the boys there start shouting right away: "Beat it; what are you butting in here for?"

"Is there a globe here?"

"What's it to you?" and a boy shoves me. I'm in a hurry and he's pushing. I wrenched away from him and say: "The principal wants to know."

Another boy who didn't hear, yells: "Are you still here? Beat it, pup, while you're still whole."

I'm confused. I don't know what to do. I try again and shout: "The principal..."

"What about the principal?"

"He wants to know if there's a globe here?"

"There's nothing here, didn't you hear?" He punched me on the head and slammed the door in my face. I really don't know, but I return and say: "They say it isn't there." But as luck would

have it, just then another pupil is coming up the corridor, carrying a globe. He's afraid that they may break it. And it seems that
there's no way for me to get to talk to the principal. I don't want
to put it off. And so, not knowing what to do, I tugged at my
teacher's sleeve. It wasn't a tug so much, only I brushed it lightly
and say: "Please Ma'am."

She heard me at once because she took me off to the side a
few paces and then bent down to me: "What is it?"

"Can you ask the principal not to have my mother come?",
I say absolutely quietly.

In fact, I said it so quietly that it seemed more like a whisper. Because it's inconvenient to be small. You always have to
raise your head. Everything occurs high up somewhere, above
you. As a result a person feels less important, degraded, weak,
and somewhat lost. Maybe that is why we like to stand beside
grownups when they are sitting: then we can look straight into
their eyes.

"Why does the principal want to see your mother?"

I don't know why, but I feel ashamed to tell her. It's awkward
to have to relate such a silly incident. I lowered my head and the
teacher bent down even more so: "You know, if I don't know the
reason, I can't ask. I have to know. Were you very naughty?"

"No", I answer. I don't know myself if that's so important.

"Then tell me."

Maybe that is why we tell things to grownups reluctantly,
because they're always in a hurry when we talk with them. It
always seems that they're not interested, that they respond only
to be rid of us faster, to be free of us sooner. Well, of course,
they have their own important affairs, and we ours. And we also
try to be brief so as not to confuse them, as if our problem is
unimportant. If only they would answer yes or no.

"Because I bumped into the principal when I was running
down the corridor."

"Did you hurt him?"

"No. I only pushed against his stomach with my hands."

She smiled at this, and in a second it was all cleared up. I
thought "thank you" to myself and make my way to my class. I
didn't even bow. That surely wasn't polite. It must have been
very impolite. Anyway, if only to be sitting on my bench again,
to have the whole thing finished.

In the last hour of school our teacher read to us about the Eskimos; that winter lasts half a year for them and that they build their houses of snow. These houses are called 'igloos'. You can light a fire in them but it still has to be pretty cold. Otherwise, the house would melt.

When I was a grownup, I also knew about Eskimos, and maybe even a little more. But they didn't interest me then. I didn't even think whether they really existed or not. But now, it is entirely different. I feel sorry for them.

It looks like I'm paying attention, with my eyes open looking at the teacher. But I see rather, fields of ice—nothing but ice and snow. Not a single little bush, not one shrub. Neither pine trees nor grass. Nothing but ice and snow. Then night comes. Wind, darkness, and sometimes a sunrise. I feel inside me the cold, the melancholy. Poor Eskimos! They have a cold life. At least, among us, even the poorest one can warm himself in the sun.

It was very quiet while the teacher read. Someone in the rear once whispered something quietly, and the teacher didn't even glance at him. But we all suddenly turned around and glared at him. Even if he was silly, and wasn't interested even in this, he shouldn't dare to interrupt. Had he tried to, he would have been sorry later.

Everyone's attention is focused on the teacher; everyone is petrified, barely blinking his eyes. For certain they are seeing, like I am, the fields of perpetual ice. It's a pity we didn't have geography before drawing. I would have drawn better. I would have drawn the eyes of the boys realistically. Although, it's true, they looked different when they weren't getting the switch. Their eyes are misty now, while before, they were full of fear. I take out my notebook, examine my triptych and stop paying attention to the reading. I got tired feeling sorry for the poor Eskimos.

It's good that I'm little again. And it's good that I'm not an Eskimo or a Chinese. How many children suffer in the world: Gypsies, Chinese, Negroes. The world is arranged in a funny way. For example: why was this one born a Negro? or, first a person is born little, then he's a grownup, then old. And finally, one day he dies. He has to die.

And suddenly, there's a big commotion in class. What is it? Why is everyone talking? But I already guessed. I knew at once what the teacher was reading about, when I wasn't listening, when I wasn't paying attention. He had to be reading about how the Eskimos hunt seals and seawolves. Of course.

Everyone is asking a question. Someone wants to know this, another that. They're even jumping out of their seats, they're so excited. But the teacher tells them to sit down, that it's noisy, and that he won't continue until it's quiet again. But they can't quiet down because each one wants to know; and everyone wants to know everything, exactly and right away.

"These Eskimos, they don't eat bread? Why don't they go where it's warm? Can't they build brick houses? Is a walrus stronger than a lion? Can an Eskimo freeze to death if he gets lost? Are there wolves there? Do they know how to read? Are there cannibals among them? Do they like white people? Do they have a king? Where do they get the nails for their sleds from?"

One of the pupils tells how his grandfather got lost in the fields. Another tells about wolves. Everyone is yelling for the other to be silent because each person wants to say something, or ask a question.

If something doesn't interest a person, then let him wait. But the children are interested in Eskimos very much. Only a short moment ago everyone was living far away, in the North Pole, and so, now, they want to know everything about the friends and neighbors and relatives whom they left there, who are having a hard time there. And they want to help them too.

In former days they used to send political prisoners to Siberia. If one of them returned from there, a lot of mothers, sisters and fiancees came from around and asked him what life was like there, what the people do there, and when will their own loved ones return. Because they can't learn much from the letters they receive, and they want to know. It's the same with us.

And it's the same with books. The teacher should tell everything he knows about seals, and snow, and reindeers, and the Aurora Borealis. He should repeat everything too because you don't hear everything when you're all excited.

For the teacher it's the fourth lesson, the fourth hour of work in school, but for the class it's news about a far-off place, about people dear to them. The teacher is tired and so are we, but in a different way. And so, this is how impatience comes about. He has had enough while we want more.

The teacher is almost angry. He threatens not to read any more as punishment. Never! It grew quiet for a moment, although they don't believe him. Had he said a week—but never! And then some silly boy starts to play the fool and says: "Oh, you won't be that mad. They're silly to be making noise, but they're good boys."

It seems like he's interrupting. It's clear at once that he wants the teacher to lose his patience. He wants to create a scene so that the teacher would start to yell. There's always someone like him. Nothing may interest him and therefore, he doesn't like it when he has to be quiet because everyone else is listening. Or else, he'll be annoying out of spite because exactly at this moment he doesn't like something.

The teacher is already looking to see whom to throw out of class. He already looked at the clock to see what time it was, because he wants the lesson to end. It's becoming unpleasant. And it really is unpleasant for the teacher because he knows that the pupils were paying attention. And so, he restrained himself, seemed to smile and then said:

"All right. You over there, the one who is being so smart, repeat what I read."

And then the usual, typical lesson begins again, during which the teacher asks questions while the class stutters and mumbles the answers incorrectly. And because of this the teacher thinks we're stupid, that we don't know anything.

When I was big, the more interested I was in something, the better I could talk about it. But maybe it's different with children. If something interests them very much, then that's the very reason it is difficult to describe it, even though they know how to. It is as if they were ashamed that they won't say it exactly as they should. It's unfortunate that in school you have to answer for grades or for praise or reproach and not according to how you feel.

The lesson ended being dull and boring and it was only during the break that we really talked about Eskimos. Someone remembers some detail better than someone else; others remember other things. And they argue: "The teacher read it that way."

"He did not."

"Maybe you were day-dreaming while he was reading."

33

"Maybe you were yourself."

They call for witnesses.

"Didn't the teacher read that they make windows from ice?"

"Isn't it true that the seal is a fish?"

"All right, let's ask the teacher then."

It's probably the same way with everyone else as it is with me. You get so lost in a thought that the rest slips by and you can't catch up afterwards. That's why somebody remembers something better than someone else. And only that way does the whole class really get to know everything.

And afterwards, outside, they play Eskimos; somewhere on the stairs or outside in the yard they tell someone who wasn't in the class everything they know; they'll even make up things from their own head to make it sound more interesting.

I was returning home with Mundek.

The street seems very exciting to me now. Everything catches my eye—the streetcars, a dog, a passing soldier, and the shops with their signs over them. Everything is new again, unfamiliar, as if freshly painted. It really isn't all new to me, because I know the streetcar, but I want to know if it has an even number or not.

"Let's guess if the first trolley has an even number, or, if the number is lower or higher than one hundred."

We're all set to play when, suddenly, we see a soldier coming. We have to look to find out if he's wearing an infantry or artillery insignia. A mechanic is working on something in a telephone booth; and workers are sweeping the gutter. One stops right away to watch—maybe it will be interesting.

New thoughts come to my mind about everything.

And a lot of dogs are to be seen about. Here's one that licks his nose with his tongue—and so, again: "Dogs don't need handkerchiefs because they can wipe their noses with their tongues, while people only sniff." And the desire to try like a dog seizes you. I reach for my nose with my tongue while Mundek says: "Push your nose down with your finger."

"It's not the same with your finger", I say.

"But try it."

And a woman passing by just then comments: "Nasty children, pointing with their tongues."

We were ashamed, because we completely forgot that people were walking and looking. But if the woman only knew what we were talking about, she wouldn't have been so surprised. It was an experiment to see how much people really need handkerchiefs, and to see how much longer a dog's tongue is, and how a person might react without a nose. We wanted to prove these things, and if someone didn't hear our conversation, he thinks we're silly.

When I was still a grownup, I was hurrying once to catch a train. And here a gust of wind suddenly blew some dust in my face. I don't know whether to hold on to my suitcase or my hat, or to shield my eyes. I'm angry and I'm hurrying so as not to be late, because there was still the ticket to buy and I was afraid that there would be a crowd at the booth. At the same time, three boys came running backwards. They're chattering away and laughing at the wind which was pushing them. And suddenly, one of them runs straight on my foot. I wanted to step aside, but he caught my suitcase too. I started yelling at them, and scolded them for creating a disturbance, for troubling people. But it's true too, that I was disturbing them. Who knows what they were playing or what they were thinking. The boy may have been playing at being a balloon or a boat or a sailing ship, while I, with my suitcase, was an underwater reef. For me—the wind was a nuisance, but for them—it was a delight. Grownups and children disturb one another.

When I was little for the first time, I liked to walk down the street with my eyes closed. I'd say: "I'll take ten steps with my eyes closed." If the street is empty, I'll keep my eyes closed for twenty steps and no matter what, I won't open them. At first, I walk very deliberately and later on, more freely. It didn't always turn out well either. Once I fell into the gutter. In those days water used to flow in those gutters, but today they have sewers and the pipes are in the ground. And so, I fell into the gutter and strained my leg—it hurt for a week. I didn't say anything at home. What was the good in that? They wouldn't have understood. They would have merely said that you ought to walk in the street with your eyes open. Of course everyone knows this, but you can try something different for a change.

Another time I banged my head against a lamp post—a big bump appeared. It's good that my cap protected me a little. If you change just one step, then the whole course changes and you either smack into a lamp post or else into a passerby. If you bump into someone, either he'll step aside and forget it or else he might say something funny and laugh. Another time, another person might get as mad as some wild animal:

"Are you blind? Don't you see?" And he'll look fiercely at you as if he wanted to eat you.

Once, when I was about fifteen years old, I was walking down the street and two little girls were chasing each other—they were running sideways somehow, when, all at once, they ran right into me. It was too late for me to avoid them and so I bent down a little—I was big then—stretched out my arms and caught them both at the same time. They looked frightened. One girl had blue eyes, and the other's were black and full of laughter. I held them both for but a brief moment, to catch my balance and then, to get by them. One of the girls shouted: "Oh!" and the other, "Excuse me." "Pardon me", I answered and they both hurried off on their way. They ran a little distance, turned around, and began laughing again, when suddenly one of them ran straight into some woman. And the woman pushed the girl so hard, that she spun around. That was rude. After all, children are needed in the world, and exactly as they are.

I say: "You want to chase after a trolley, Mundek?"

We just happened to be standing then at the trolley stop. "Okay," he says.

"Let's see who's faster—us or the trolley. Up to the corner."

"To the corner."

It's easy at first, because the trolley doesn't have much speed. But afterwards, we're chasing it in the middle of the street along the path where the horses go; then, a carriage gets in our way. We lost.

"But I was first", Mundek says.

And I: "That's not fair; your coat was open on the bottom."

"But who was stopping you? You could have pulled your coat up."

I forgot, of course. It's been so long since I raced with trolley cars that I fell out of practice. "Okay", I say. "Let's try again, only this time I'll unbutton my coat." But he doesn't want to any more. He says that it ruins his shoes.

While I would only run. I'm glad that I don't get tired. I was already panting and my heart was pounding, but I stopped for a moment and now, I'm all rested again. A child's fatigue doesn't exhaust you.

We talk about how to jump on and off a trolley. It isn't dangerous at all. Only, you have to know how to do it. You have to start by chasing after a trolley, even one that's far away. If you know how, you have to run alongside it and and be able to touch it with your hand. That's the moment you reach out and only then—but not at full speed, and only while the trolley is moving—you hop on and then off again. You can learn in a month. And it's better to use the back car, because even if you should fall down, you wouldn't fall under the wheels. And you have to look around to see if a car's there or not.

Grownups break their legs too.

We started to talk about accidents.

"In my time there were no cars." I say.

Mundek looked at me surprised: "How's that, there weren't any?"

"There weren't any." I say, annoyed at myself that it slipped out so.

We stopped near a bill-board with some posters on it.

'Katy's Love' is playing in the movies.

"Would you like to see it?"

Mundek made a grimace. "No. Love pictures are dumb. They're either kissing or else they're walking around their rooms. Only once in a while someone shoots. I prefer mysteries."

"Would you like to be a detective?"

37

"I think so. You run over rooftops and fences with a Brauning."

We read the circus posters.

"I like circuses the best."

We stand there a while chattering, and then move on.

"Tomorrow we have five lessons."

"Biology."

"If only the teacher would tell us more about seals and polar bears.

"Would you like to be a bear?"

"You bet."

"But bears are clumsy."

"That's not so. It only seems that way. But I'd rather be an eagle. I'd soar up to the top of the highest mountain, higher than the clouds. I'd be all by myself and proud."

It's more pleasant to have wings than to fly an aeroplane. You always need gasoline, or it may break down, or else, you need hangers to store it in. And then, you can't land everywhere. And you have to keep it clean and warm up the motor before taking off. But wings—if you're not flying, you merely fold them up.

If people had wings they'd have to dress differently. The shirts would have to have openings in the back and you would have to hold your wings on your back, or else under your jacket.

Two boys are walking along the street—as if nothing— talking. The same ones who, only a while ago, were sticking out their tongues to lick their noses, the same ones who, just now were chasing after trolley cars. And now they're talking about wings for people.

Grownups think that children can only manage to be mischievous, or are only able to recite the table of threes but it is really they who foretell the distant future, argue about it, and debate it. Grownups will say that people will never have wings; but I was a grownup once and I say that they could have them.

And so, Mundek and I are talking and saying that it would be pleasant to fly to and from school. I'd fly out of the classroom and when I'd get tired, I'd walk a little. One time my wings will rest, another time, my legs. You could even lean out of the window and perch on the roof, and you could fly to the woods for a picnic. We fly in pairs over the city, but beyond it, each one goes his own way. In the woods you could walk wherever you wanted to and if you got lost, you could fly up in the air and find the picnic spot—you couldn't get lost then.

"What do you think, Mundek, wouldn't it be great?"

"You bet it would."

And people would sharpen their eyesight. They say that migrating birds can find their way back to their villages and nests. They have neither maps nor compasses and they can manage their way over oceans, mountains, and rivers.

Birds are smart—smarter than people. But man rules over everything; everything obeys him.

"But maybe that's so because he kills the best and not because he is the best."

We got to thinking about things and here, suddenly, a boy is passing by—a big bully—and he knocked my cap off my head. He had a stick and he knocked it off with it. I run up to him right away: "What are you starting?"

"Did I do something to you?" he says, pretending surprise.

"You knocked my cap off."

"What cap?" He laughs shamelessly and pretends in full view.

"Are you saying that you didn't knock it off?"

"That's right, I didn't. Look, he's holding your cap."

In the meantime, Mundek picked up my cap and is waiting to see what will happen.

"He's holding it, but you knocked it off."

"Beat it, smarty pants or I'll knock it off again. As if I don't have anything else to do."

"You bet you don't, you big ape. You won't let us pass quietly."

"Hey! Only watch out with that 'ape' stuff, or you might really get it." And he nicked me under my chin with his stick. But I grabbed the stick quickly and broke it. He comes up close to me, but I'm standing pat.

"Either you give me back my stick or else, you pay for it."

He didn't bend down though. He was much taller and so, I jumped up a little and hit him with my fist in the head. But his cap didn't fall off.

I took to my heels and Mundek is right behind me. And did we run!

"Good for you", I thought, "the next time don't butt in, because you can get it even from a little person."

At first, he started to chase after us, but then he saw that it didn't make any sense, that he didn't happen to pick on a sissy, and so he left off chasing us.

We stopped and laughed aloud.

A second ago I was so angry that I saw the color red. Now I'm happy again. I dust off my cap with my sleeve.

"Why did you start it with him?" Mundek asks.

"Did I or did he?"

"He did, of course, but he's bigger."

"He's bigger, so that means that he can bang people around?"

"And what if he recognizes you tomorrow and wallops you?"

"He won't, don't worry. Why should he?"

Mundek is right though. Now I'll have to be on guard.

But is it possible that in broad daylight, on a busy street, hats can be knocked off heads? If it happened to a grownup, there would be a big scandal, a crowd of people, a policeman. But because it happened to a child, it means nothing. There are trouble-makers among children and we don't have any help against them, or protection—we have to manage on our own.

We stand there on the corner and regret that we have to part. We were talking about something important when this bully interfered. The walk home was pleasant; we played and even had a little fight.

Now I'm going alone and I'm trying to walk in such a way as to step only in the middle of the pavement stones. It's like playing hop-scotch—you try to stay off the lines. It would be a simple thing but you have to watch out for pedestrians; and to make one step after another without stepping on a line isn't always so easy. I begin to count. Once I managed—two, three, four. I can still go higher—five, six. I'm all tense. But such excitement is fun in games.

I only stopped eight times before reaching my gate. And I managed to scare a cat in front of the store near my house too. He jumped to the side and stared at me and then raised his paw in a funny way.

"Were you asked anything in class?" Mama asks.

"No."

I kissed her hand—so tenderly that Mama looked at me and stroked my head.

I'm glad that the principal forgave me and that I have a mother again. Children imagine that a grownup doesn't need a mother, that only children can be orphans. But it's this way that the older people get, less and less frequent is it that they have parents. Oh, and how many moments does a grownup suffer when he longs for his mother or father who, it seems to him, are the only ones who would listen to him and, if need be, forgive him, and feel sorry for him. And so, a grownup can feel like an orphan too.

I had my lunch; but what will I do now?

I go out into the yard. Felek, Michael, and Wacek are there.

Do we play at hunting?

Michael carved out a pistol, painted it with black ink, and decorated it with nails. He got hold of some nails with golden heads—of course, not real gold—they were brass and shiny. Michael called it the 'hero's' pistol. He made believe that he got it as a reward for valour on the field of battle. The general himself presented it to him for a courageous deed. And after the battle, the whole division lined up in his honor for a review. The band is playing, there are flags—and the soldiers all shout cheers. After the review, the general says: "My ancestor captured this pistol in Turkey long ago, and it has come down to me through the male line of my family, from father to son. It was in our family for two hundred years. And now, because you saved my life, I want it to serve you."

This is Michael's story. Once he said that it happened near Vienna, another time near Cecora, or else at Grunwald. But that isn't important. Now that I'm a child again, it seems to me that history is unimportant, or the facts a person knows. What is really important, is how a person feels inside. When I was a teacher, I felt differently.

And so, Michael's going to be a hunter. Felek is the rabbit while Wacek and I are dogs. We didn't decide on this all at once. At first, there was going to be a chase after a robber, while I wanted to lead an expedition to the Eskimos.

It rarely happens that everyone has the same plan. Sometimes someone doesn't feel like playing very much and so, you have to give in, to encourage him. They don't want to play Eskimos because there's no snow, while Mundek won't let us play cops and robbers: "The last time we played that you tore off my sleeve."

We didn't tear it off exactly, only it was sewn on so lightly that the thread gave way. Michael was a dangerous criminal and we were taking him to the cellar to be imprisoned. He was trying to break away and escape and so, we couldn't pay attention to his sleeve.

Playing at being a rabbit is quieter that's true, but if it goes off well, it can be a lot of fun too. The most important thing in a game is the person with whom you choose to play. Some boys are so wild that it's clear at once that the game's going to end in some accident. That kind of a person doesn't have any regard for anything, everything has to be his way; he has to always come out on top. It isn't very pleasant with such a person because you have to be careful. You invite him to play, otherwise he'll cause trouble, but then you have to give him certain conditions. It's also unpleasant to play with someone who is quarrelsome. The slightest thing and he starts arguing or else takes offense. Boys take offense rarely, but girls do often. At the most exciting moment in the game, he'll start an argument over nothing: "Then I'm not playing." Everyone can say that he's wrong, but he persists in his own. If you can, you give in to him, not to have everything spoiled. But that only makes you angry. And grownups don't understand. They will say: "Go and play. Why aren't you playing with him?" or else, "All right, you've played enough."

And they're angry when we don't obey.

But really, how can you play with a clumsy person, someone who will fall down right away, start crying, and then go home and complain? Or else, with a silly person who doesn't understand anything, and who will spoil the game at the most exciting moment? How can you interrupt and break a game off suddenly, and then not know how it would have ended? A game has to be well planned and it doesn't always turn out well. But if it does succeed, then you would like to enjoy it.

And so, we're playing at hunting...

The rabbit darted around the yard, and the dogs chased after him from opposite directions. Then he makes a dash into the shadows. But I'm right after him. I stop and sniff. Did he go up the stairs or down the cellar? It seems to me that I hear something rustling in the cellar. I slink low since it's dark there. The rabbit almost always runs into the cellar because it's always easier to crouch down there and hide in the darkness. And if you wanted the game to be a little quieter, then it's better in the cellar too, because you always have to be a little more careful, and you're afraid that you might bump into something or someone.

Last year Olek knocked Joe's mother, who was carrying a bushel of coal, off the steps. He was running real hard and bumped into her. I was a grownup then and I even remember how shocked I felt over the fact that children could allow themselves so much, and that the janitor allowed them to play in the yard. The boys are all so wild and the tenants have no peace. It's fortunate that the woman didn't injure herself, that she only scratched her leg. But it could have been much worse.

We had the greatest sympathy whenever a grownup got a bump or a black-and-blue mark; but if something happens to a child we say: "Serves you right. Next time don't fight." As if a child feels less, or has different skin. It's all right if they only laugh at you, even though this makes you angry too; but you hurt yourself and got scared, and they're joking. It's worse sometimes too—they'll scold you even. They know that it wasn't done on purpose. Who would want to hurt himself deliberately? Though it appears as if: "I'll hurt myself just to make you angry."

Now I understand that if I'm a hunting dog and a rabbit is hiding in the cellar in the darkness there somewhere, I can't go down one step at a time—I have to jump down three steps at a time, even if I were to slip and bump my head or else, get a splinter in my hand. I want to catch him. In that case, I gamble and I don't stop to think at all. Simply, I want to catch him. And doesn't it often happen that a real hunting dog will dash into a forest at such a great speed and crack his skull against a tree? And a dog has four legs while I have only two.

I'm a dog and I'm barking and whining because I've lost the scent. When I was a grownup, I had a deep voice and I couldn't bark at all, or crow like a cock, or cackle like a chicken. But now I recovered the child's clear, thin voice and I bark as of old.

I stand poised for a brief moment and then rush down into the cellar. Wacek's right behind me. But here, suddenly, the rabbit darts over our heads from above us and dashes out into the yard.

We agreed beforehand that you couldn't go out into the street. But it's cramped in the courtyard and so, the rabbit ran around it a couple of times and then saw the hunter and his dogs closing in on him from all sides.

And then the rabbit makes a dash for the gate.

"That's not allowed!"

But try to tell a rabbit when it's running for its life what's allowed and what isn't. It's protecting its very life. And if we want to continue playing, we understand this. There's always an agreement before a game on what is allowed and what isn't but it's always hard to stick to the rules in the case of real danger. If we're tired, or if we don't feel like playing very much, or if someone does something that's absolutely forbidden, then you interrupt the game at once and a quarrel begins. It's not really a quarrel but it's just enough of a break to let you rest a little, or to change something in the game, to introduce something better. Either someone is dropped from the game and you take on someone else, or else the dog becomes the rabbit or maybe it's decided that you can't go there or that this isn't the way.

This is really one of the reasons why it's fun to play by yourself, without grownups. The grownup, ahead of time, says how everything should be, himself chooses who should be what, and makes everyone hurry up, as if he were wasting his time. But he really doesn't know boys.

It's good to argue in a game too. You can rest a little then. Everyone gets together in a huddle and deliberates. It happens that someone gets hit or someone's clothes are torn and then the whole blame is put on the one who was playing against the rules that were agreed upon ahead of time.

"It's your fault."

He defends himself, that it's not he, but he feels guilty nevertheless. And we know that it's unpleasant to admit being at fault unless, of course, one goes too far, or else, is too troublesome.

"C'mon that's enough now."

"Are we going to play or not?"

"O.K., O.K. Let's start then."

"Stop your arguing."

"Who doesn't want to play, can leave."

And so, the rabbit darts for the gate and in a moment is in the street. And we're right behind him. He crosses over to the other side and we cross over after him. It's easier for us, because if one of us slows down, the other comes up from the side and scares him. We run straight, while he zigzags. But we chase well, seeing that the rabbit is some two years older, is stronger and runs faster. We'll catch him in the end, but the whole point is how long will he defend himself.

Finally, we caught him on the third floor of a house. He was exhausted and was panting hard. We caught him alive. He didn't even put up a fight. He just gave up.

Then we sat down on the steps and talked. We were tired too, because we ran upstairs. Only we told ourselves that no matter what, he won't get away, that we would catch him. He could have hidden in his house, his den, but he didn't live here. Then he says: "If I wanted to, you wouldn't have caught me."

"And we could have caught you sooner, only we didn't want to kill you. We felt sorry for you."

"Sorry, my eye! You didn't even give me a chance to rest. Even a real dog doesn't chase that way."

"Then why did you run into the street when it wasn't allowed?"

"Why not? Where could I run to?"

"You could have given yourself up."

"That's smart? You should have fired. Had you wounded me, you would have had me. He's holding the gun and doesn't shoot. Some hunter!"

That's true. Michael should have fired. And he was chasing too. He forgot that he was the hunter and not a dog. That was a mistake. Had he fired, Felek would have fallen down, since he was already exhausted. He would have given up with honor. Michael was annoyed.

"He got the pistol from the general himself at Cecora, and he couldn't manage to fire at a rabbit. Some hero!"

Michael was offended: "If you're going to laugh, then I won't tell you anything."

Wacek was afraid that they would start to fight, and therefore said: "Remember when we were playing the tigers that escaped from the circus, and I was the hero?"

We started to talk about the trained animals we had seen, about lions that jump through fiery hoops, about an elephant that rode a bicycle, about monkeys and dogs. It's more exciting to talk about dogs, because each of us had seen them himself, whereas we had only heard or read about the others.

Felek's uncle has a dog that obeys, retrieves, plays dead, and doesn't let you touch him. Then there was the soldier who came home on leave and who had a trained dog. He did a lot of different tricks with him in the yard. He showed the boys his bayonet and told us about automatic rifles and about bombs.

"If there were a war, I'd join the infantry right away."

"First ask if they'd take you!"

46

He's too small. Then a sigh.

Next we talked about water-sprites too; that they have webbed feet like ducks and that they rescue drowning people. And we talked about drowning men too. It already got dark, and it was scary to go on talking.

"The teacher read to us about Eskimos in school today."

We talk about Eskimos and about school.

How good it would be if real explorers and discoverers and soldiers came and talked in schools about what they do and what they had seen.

"Once, the teacher was telling us about her trip to the Tatra mountains, and about a storm and lightening. You talk about it completely differently if you've seen it, and another way if it's out of a book. It's less interesting the other way."

"Yeh, explorers tell about their trips, but only to grownups. You think such important people are going to talk to children? It isn't worth it."

We grew silent. The watchman lights the lamp on the stairs. He sees us and starts chasing us away. "What are you doing here in the dark? Hurry off, home!"

And he looks around suspiciously as if, for certain, we were doing something we weren't supposed to. He probably thought that we were smoking cigarettes because there was a match on the ground. First he looked at it, then at us in turn.

Maybe it only seems so to us, but distrust is an awful thing. And grownups are even in the habit of taking this opportunity to correct us on other things. If they don't happen to notice anything then it's all right; but if they should see something, then it's always:

"Button yourself up; why are your shoes covered with mud? Did you do your homework? Show me your ears. Trim your fingernails."

And little by little, this teaches us to avoid, to hide—even if you haven't done anything bad. And if they should glance at us accidentally, then we immediately wait for some comment from them. Maybe that's why we don't like teachers' pets. Maybe he isn't really a teacher's pet, but rather, because he mingles with grownups too freely; he isn't afraid of their glances and so, appears to be in agreement with them.

When I was a teacher, I did the same thing. It seemed to me then that it was a good thing that I noticed everything and commented on every little thing. But now, I think differently: a child ought to feel at ease when you look at him. And if you really want to say something to him, then it shouldn't appear that it occurred to you accidentally but, rather, that you really want to tell him something.

And so, we're sitting on the stairs in the dark. And how should we have been sitting, since the lamps weren't lit? We were just talking. And if we say that we were, for certain they'll answer: "What could you have been talking about there now? About something silly, no doubt."

Of course not about clever things. But then, do grownups always talk wisely? Why show scorn right away?

It seems to grownups that they know us well. What can there be of interest in a child? He's lived only a short time; he knows little, and understands little. Certainly, everyone forgets about what kind of a child he was and thinks that now he's the smartest.

"Come on. Go home. Hurry up!"

We parted reluctantly, slowly, step by step—in a way that he shouldn't get the idea that we're afraid of him. Because if we really wanted to stay and do what we weren't supposed to, then he wouldn't have been able to keep an eye on all of us—and if not here, then somewhere else, and if not now, then later.

Supper wasn't ready yet at home, and so I began to play with little Irene. I have a little sister. Yes, and a mother and father. And little Irene.

We play a game where I shut my eyes and cover my ears and face the wall, while she hides her doll. Then I try to find it. And when I find it, I pretend that I don't want to return it and I hold it high over my head. Then she pulls my arm and cries:

"Give me back my doll. Give it back."

She has to say this fifteen or twenty times, because that's the ransom. If I were to find the doll right away, then it's less; but if I looked for it for a long time, then it's more. Once, she hid the doll under the pillow and I found it right away. She only had to cry "Give me back my doll" ten times.

Another time she hid it in a coat pocket; a third time it was behind a chest-of-drawers. A fourth time she hid it under the bed. And when she hid it in a pail, I had to look for it for a long time and then she had to cry thirty times before I gave it back.

Children's games aren't silly; to uncover a secret, to find the hidden object, to show that something can't be so well hidden that you can't find it—that's the whole point. The harder it is to find something, the more fun it is. Whether it's the truth of grownups, their discoveries and inventions and knowledge—or a doll in a pail or under a window. The whole of nature—that's little Irene hiding her doll, while mankind, searching in toil, that's me, a little boy. I was chasing a rabbit a while ago with all the speed and deftness my legs could muster while here, I'm uncovering a doll with shrewdness, cunning, and persistence. What else do we do in life; what does the whole of mankind accomplish? We chase after rabbits and hunt for dolls.

I'm even tired with this long day and I want to go to bed as quickly as possible.

"Why are you so quiet?" Papa asks. "Did you misbehave in school?"

"No", I answer, "My head aches."

"Maybe you'd like some lemon?" Mama asks.

I washed only my hands and face, quickly undressed, and am lying in bed with my eyes shut.

The first day that I'm little again has ended. And how many things there were in this single day! I only wrote down a few of the things which I was able to recall from memory—those things which lasted longer.

If a man is deluged with impressions that resemble a spring downpour, can he recall and describe all the drops? Will the lapping waves of a flooded river let themselves be counted?

I was an Eskimo and a dog; I chased and was chased; I was a champion and also a hapless victim in an accident; an artist and a philosopher—life sounds to me like an orchestra.

And I understand why a child can be a ripe musician, and that when we examine carefully his talk or drawings and when, finally, he begins trusting himself and starts expressing himself and we penetrate his unique and worthy being—then we'll find in him a master of feelings, a poet, and an artist. This will happen. Only we aren't really grownup yet. We are still much too involved in the material life.

Today, I carried out an expedition to the land of eternal snow; I was transformed into a dog with glistening fangs, and more; lots more...

When I was playing with little Irene, the doll wasn't merely a doll, but the ransom of a crime, a hidden body which had to be tracked. And when I found it, I took it carefully like a dead body.

The doll was a drowning person and I, a fisherman. Rocking sideways, I went around the room moving my arms as if they were a net.

The doll was a bandit: Where is it hiding? I moved around the room cautiously, crouching, so as not to get a fatal shot. Not in the pocket of a coat or under a pillow did it hide, but rather, in a big forest, in an underground lair, in a swamp or on the bottom of the ocean.

I didn't tell Irene, because she's small. She wouldn't have understood anyway. That was my own private game.

I forgot to add that Mama happened to come into the room when we were playing.

"Give her back her doll. Why are you annoying her?"

"We're playing this way. It's a game."

"You may be playing, but she's getting angry. You could hear her cries on the stairs."

I also imagined some sort of white object in the corner of the cellar, as if it were a man without a head and covered by a shroud. And when I was running out of the cellar, for a brief moment I wasn't chasing after a rabbit, but rather, was running away from a ghost. It only lasted a moment, but my chest was pounding, and before my eyes I saw three dark flashes.

I didn't write abut how thirsty I was during the lesson. The teacher though, didn't let me leave.

"The bell will ring soon. You can get a drink then."

He was right. But I'm a child; I have a different clock; I measure time differently, have a different calendar. My day, which is divided into short seconds and long centuries, lasts forever. It wasn't only for ten minutes that I was thirsty.

"When will the bell ring? Because I'm suffering. My mouth is burning, my eyes and thoughts are burning. I'm really suffering, because I'm a child."

I didn't write that during the recess my friend let me play his new harmonica—just to try it, to see if it was a good one. He was boasting that it was the best and that it wouldn't rust. I played it for about a minute, wiped it on my jacket and gave it back. And that was all. Of course, that wasn't really 'all', because if he should lose his harmonica, exchange or sell, or break it, and I should have my own in half a year, he might ask me to let him use mine, and I'd remember and let him. And if I shouldn't give it to him, then he would be right in saying: "Just look at the kind you are. And I let you." Such favors you remember if you're going to be an honest person.

I didn't mention either that I have an extra long coat—to grow into. It got in my way when I raced the trolley car. Until I grow up, it will always be getting in my way, no matter how often I wear it.

Again, it isn't such a little thing because do I know how long it will last? Half a year, a year, forever?

I didn't mention that I suddenly spotted a live fly on the window pane. I was glad to see it and I went and got a little sugar secretly from the cupboard and threw a few grains to it. I was feeling spring. Just let little Irene or anyone harm it.

I found a bottle cork. It will come in handy. I have it in my pants pocket, near my bed. I also saw a soldier on the street. I made a few marching steps and I saluted. He smiled at me in a friendly way.

I washed my face with ice cold water. I enjoyed it like swimming—good, cold water—a fleeting joy.

When I was a grownup, I had an old rug which was faded and worn. And once, walking in a street, I saw the same kind of rug in a shop window, with the same pattern of flowers in it. Only it was brand new. Somehow, I walked past the shop more slowly and with my head a little bowed.

When I was a grownup, they came into my room after the long winter to wash the windows. After so many months the windows were very dirty. And when I returned home from work later in the day, I stood in front of the window for a long time and looked through the sparkling glass with real pleasure.

When I was a grownup, I once met an uncle of mine on the street. I hadn't seem him in a very long time and I had all but forgotten him. He was walking alone, so white, and leaning on his cane. He asked me how things were going.

"I'm getting old, Uncle", I said to him.

"What, already? And what should I say then? Why, you're a mere lad yet!"

I was glad that he was still living and that he called me by my name.

And here, suddenly, a warm hand touches my forehead. I tremble and then open my eyes. The uneasy glance of my mother meets my eyes.

"Are you sleeping?"

"No."

"Does your head hurt?"

"No."

"Are you cold? Should I cover you?"

Her hand touches my face and chest. I sit up.

"Don't worry, Mama. My head didn't hurt at all."

"But you said it did."

"It seemed to. I only wanted to sleep."

I embrace her around her neck and hug her and look into her eyes. Then I quickly dive under the covers. I could still hear her voice:

"Sleep, son."

I'm little again, and Mama calls me "son". And again the window panes are sparkling, and again the rug appears new and bright in its old, former colors. Again I have young hands, young legs, young bones and blood, young breath, tears, and joys.

Joys, tears, and a young prayer, a child's prayer.

And I feel asleep, as if after a long march...

52

The Second Day

At night it snowed. It's so white outside—so very white.

I haven't seen snow in many years. After so many, many years, I'm glad that it snowed, that it's white all over again.

It's true that grownups like nice weather too, but they only think and ponder over it while we, it seems, drink it in. Grownups too, like a bright morning, but for us it is a frozen wine—it's as if we were made drunk by it.

When I was a grownup and I saw snow, I already anticipated the slush that would follow. I felt the damp overshoes and wondered whether there would be enough coal for the winter. And joy—it was there too, but sprinkled somehow with ashes, dusty and grey. But now I feel only that white, transparent and blinding joy. Why? For no reason at all: because it snowed!

I walk slowly, carefully; it's a pity to trample on it. All about it sparkles and shines and glitters; it changes and plays and is alive. And there are thousands of little sparks inside me. It's as if someone sprinkled diamond dust in my soul and along the ground. The dust was sown and now diamond trees will spring up and a wondrous fairy tale will be born.

A tiny, white star falls on my hand, a beautiful, precious little star. It's a pity that it will disappear, be scared away. It's a shame—or else, I'll blow on it myself and be glad that it disappears because another one appears. I open my mouth and catch the little stars with my tongue. I feel the crystal cold of the snow, its clean and cold whiteness.

And when the snow melts, icicles will appear. You can knock them down with your hand. You can catch the falling drops with your lips. With a strong sweep of your arm, you rake them up from under a cornice: they fall and shatter with a frozen sound.

Truly, it's winter and it's spring.

This isn't snow; it's the sorcerer's kingdom of the magic-colored soap bubble.

And snowballs. Balls, pills—mischief, surprise; snowballs—as many as you would want! You don't buy them, you don't borrow them, you don't ask for them. You have them. You squeeze them, or they hit something lightly and fall apart. That's nothing—right away you'll have another one. He throws at you, you at him, at his back, his arm or hat—and nothing. Only laughter and a fluttering heart.

You fall down and pretend to dust yourself off. Some snow gets down your collar—b-r-r—it's cold but exciting. It's an adventure. You begin to roll a snowball. It shapes evenly and starts to grow. You choose a good spot on the ground and push the snowball over it. It grows bigger. Not with your palm now but with your whole hand—you feel it getting heavier. You slipped and you slow down—you move more carefully now. Whose is bigger? But now what? Make a snow-man, or jump on it with your feet and smash it?

The workmen will shovel the snow into piles along the sides of the streets and so, down the middle you roam, up to your knees in the white down.

Gee, I need some boards and nails! The most necessary thing, the most important thing in the whole world—beyond this nothing exists—one's own sled, lined on the bottom with a piece of metal! What to do here? What to take apart? or find? or beg for?—to get some boards. Ice-skates too. And if you can't have a pair, then even one will do. A person feels like an orphan without a sled or skates.

Such are our white cares, our white desires. I'm sorry for you, grownups, that you are so meager of the joy of snow which wasn't yesterday!

The wind garnered up the little stars from the roof-tops, wainscots, and gutters and dumped the white powder in the street. A cold, white cloud. Up and down through squinting eyes, a curtain of white eyelashes. There's only the street. Not a forest or a field—only the white street and the excited, young cry of joy. Little figures of people will begin to appear on the roofs of houses soon, and with shovels they'll begin to throw the snow down onto the fenced-off paths below. And you'll feel envious, that it's high up, that they can fall but don't, that such work is easy and exciting and beautiful; to push the snow from on high—and the passersby make way and look up.

If I were a king, I would order on the first day of winter, instead of a thousand school bells, as a signal, twelve cannon shots, to announce that school has been closed.

There are boxes and crates and boards in the cellar or attic of every school.

It's the holiday of the first sleigh rides.

The trolleys will stop running and all motor traffic will be forbidden. Our sleds with their bells will take possession of the city. All the streets, squares and gardens will belong to us. The White Holiday of the school children—the day of the first snow.

This was my way.

Instead—it's only school now. I know that it isn't her fault, but I feel sad. What else? Five hours in my seat—reading, and solving problems.

"Please, Ma'am, there's snow."

"Isn't it so, Ma'am?"

At first she calms you down gently; then, later, more sternly. She gets annoyed, but she can't deny it; she feels, of course, that we're right. That's how it is.

"Please, Ma'am."

"Be quiet."

Then the usual will follow: "Who'll say another word, or complain... It's the last time I'm going to tell you."

She'll begin to threaten.

And so it's our fault again? We're to blame? It's not the snow's fault, but ours; it's always our fault.

We were asleep—at night—we didn't even know; we can bring proof from our parents; it fell itself from the sky and if we're not allowed to say it, if we have to pretend that we didn't see it, that we don't know; or, if it's wrong and nasty that we do know and are glad even, well, it's too bad. So be it.

Only one boy is standing in the corner.

I'll quiet down with the class. A few uneasy glances out the window, and a last look of hope at the teacher, that maybe... And now silence. Only the lesson now.

There are no cannon shots to announce the white holiday for the school children.

Someone is saying something uninteresting.

I open my pen case and count the number of nibs I have. I take them out, try one, write with it, but it's too thick. Twelve nibs. And that's all. They're saying something dull about some boy, some farmer. I yawn.

"You shouldn't yawn during the lesson." My neighbor nudges me to stand up. I rise. I realize now that I yawned and that the teacher is addressing me:

"Sit straight; don't slouch!"

I sit straight. I don't slouch. I yawn secretly.

"Look at the blackboard, please."

I look at the blackboard and see that it's snowing outside the window; but I'm not interested in it anymore. I sit quietly.

"Repeat."

What?

"Go and stand in the corner. You're not paying attention."

I walk slowly to the corner, deliberately.

"Hurry up."

Someone laughed. Often someone will laugh like that in class for no reason at all. And then it happens that everyone else will join in with him.

My legs begin to hurt. They don't hurt exactly, but they're giving way. It seems strange. There's enough energy for racing and sledding and ice-skating. But now—it isn't spite or stubbornness or laziness; it isn't the mischievous school-boy spite, but a sincere, honest and painful "I can't." As if someone took my legs in his hands and broke them—like a stick.

It's a stern punishment—the corner. I'm weak; sitting in my seat bothered me; I leaned back; I couldn't sit straight. Now I have to stand.

I console myself:

"It's better in the corner. If the class starts to misbehave, I won't share the common blame."

And that could happen, because, beneath the silence, there smoulders a hidden wound, a desire for revenge which is only waiting for a signal. Will a dare-devil be found or not? Because if only one person starts something now, it won't end in a small disorder. I know this.

And so, someone drove a pen nib into his desk, pulled it back a little and then, released it. It hum-m-ms. The teacher hasn't heard it, but we did—from the very first, faint attempt. It's hard to catch such a person, because he drove the nib deep into a panel and he has only to touch it, and right away—z-i-n-g! Now it's louder.

"Who's humming?"

There's no answer.

Now two of them are at it, alternating.

When will the lesson be over, finally? Why, it just can't go on forever. If only there were a clock on the wall. And why isn't there one? Why is it that the teacher knows and only we are hopeless, in despair?

"I'm asking, who is humming? Olszewski, is it you?"

"What? I don't know anything."

"Who then?"

"I don't know anything and right away you're on me."

The class begins to awaken from its sleep. It's becoming interesting. We are waiting for new and more daring strumming now. The teacher already guessed what was up. Now a third one will join in, to confuse her. He's probably taking his nib out at this very moment, is making an innocent face, and is inserting the nib in the wood.

"Put your hands behind you, class."

The bell finally! Understand now why the school, with a certain amount of shame it's true, requires that the hands be kept folded on the desks and that we leave the room in pairs.

Because we'd make a dash for the door—a swarm, a horde, a whirlwind.

School doors should be wide in case of a fire or for such snow days. We push and hurry so as not to lose a single moment. We have to escape, but we have so much distance, so many obstacles: narrow doors, a tight corridor, stairs, the vestibule. And we all have to be first in the yard. And so, with elbows and knees and chest and head, we pave the way—we're out of breath, our hands burn from the cold snow.

Something whizzes past your eyes—already!

The first snowball; it doesn't matter what kind, and—bang!— at the first person the better. He won't be angry. Such a wondrous and exciting game it will be. And no one, absolutely no one interferes. They don't dare. They don't risk it.

The janitor knows that his steps will get muddied. The teachers took refuge in the office and are smoking their cigarettes. The teachers pretend that they don't know, because it wouldn't do any good. These are our ten minutes and in their defense we're an avalanche, a hurricane, all the elements converging.

Soon there's a snowball fight at very close quarters—an arm's length—a free-for-all. It's a fight where there are no enemies, where you don't want to hurt anyone but, nevertheless, you have to come out the winner. You don't count the blows you receive or give; you don't check the accuracy of your throws, and you don't feel the blows on your back. Only to hold your stand until the end.

Someone fell too hard; someone's inspecting something—a wound on his shirt or pants, and the first tears. We don't see the wound; we don't feel sorry for him.

Only the most terrible thing can interrupt our play: maybe something like a broken window or the sight of real blood. Who knows though, if this would stop the fight right away—and maybe it would only be a momentary break.

There is no plan to the game, no leader. Everyone's together and everyone's on his own against everybody else. Only by chance are there alliances, but they are fleeting.

Here, three of us are pouring it on a single one. We've cornered him against the wall. He's used up all the snow under him and now, not with snowballs because he's not fast enough, but rather with just the harmless powder is he fighting; and he can't bend down because we're standing right up against him, chest to chest.

"Do you surrender?"

"No!"

He's right. Because one of the three suddenly threw a snowball at one of his own allies. Betrayal—panic in attack. It's not a betrayal at all, but a signal to break up and dash off to a more interesting place.

He's right not to have surrendered, because in the last moment rescue comes. Suddenly we feel a heap of snowballs on our undefended back. And he escapes in the confusion, weakened, all white from head to foot, but unconquered.

Or, one of the three of his attackers with a hastily made snowball, a handful of powder snow, forces it in his mouth or else, rubs his face with it and scratches him with a little stone that was hidden in the snow. Of course, it's not allowed but, then, what kind of rules can there be in battle?

Or else, we disband suddenly, not knowing with or against whom we were fighting. We get mixed up. Familiar faces are racing past, half-familiar ones noticed on the run, and completely unknown ones. We struggle not against man, but against time. Every moment must be used to advantage—every fraction of each second is precious. Every moment used up, squeezed, sucked up to the last drop of the joy of movement.

And here, suddenly, both of us are lying in the snow. I'm on top. And already, on purpose, I give way, to give him a chance to get even, to be under him for a moment. For a moment. He understood, then we get up and run together, holding hands or else, we go off in separate directions.

One goal: to endure all the possible situations of the fight. To enjoy and imbibe the most sensations. To strain every fiber of muscle and nerve. To breathe from the deepest corner of your lungs. To pump for the thousandth time through your heart the heavy wave of blood.

Because we, too, are capable of getting lost in bliss—not scarlet but white. And nothing will be forgotten. And in the weariness of the following school hour, we will digest one by one the moments of those wonderful adventures, those powerful sensations.

Children grow—that's really true isn't it? Their bodies and souls grow? I'd like to prove scientifically that they grow the most during these recesses. To show this beyond a doubt.

But here's the bell. No matter. All the better. The bell adds drive to the game—like a band does for a company of soldiers

60

on a march. If we were conserving a tiny bit of energy before the bell, then now it's just the opposite. To the last drop, to the very bottom, the very end—absolutely—every bit of strength—like a dance at white heat—to plunge headlong into the very thick of the battle.

The deciding, dangerous, and unconscious moment. At this moment, when all calculation and consideration are gone—at this very moment, windows are most frequently broken, snowballs are thrown very hard and recklessly, a leg is broken. Here, suddenly, a short, unexpected and stubborn fight can be started—not because you don't like the other boy, or because you're getting even with him for something that happened yesterday—but because the bell is summoning you to class. Accidentally he pushed you or punched you. You would have overlooked this before the bell; you wouldn't even have taken notice of it. But now, because the bell rang, you feel it, and you won't let it pass. You're surprised yourself afterwards, and ashamed even, and you even regret it. Your friends feel sorry for you too, and they regret it themselves that they didn't ward off the fight in time.

It's a pity that the wonderful game was spoiled so.

Wonderful?!

How meager is man's language. But then, what can you say?

If I were the janitor, I would ring the bell for a long time, in such snowy recesses. Because, as long as he's ringing the bell, we don't know anything—the peal of the bell incites us to play. Only when the ringing stops—in that first moment of silence following—the game is already illegal, unenthusiastic. The sides already begin to break up, the more disciplined ones begin to withdraw; you notice the hesitation in the movements, the uncertainty in the eyes, you lose confidence, you aren't sufficiently sure of yourself—you know that you have to concede, but that's equal to defeat, desertion, betrayal.

It's silent, but in a second the air will be filled with the sound of the second bell. And then it will be too late.

We run for the vestibule. We'll probably be stopped there carefully by the one who's in charge of keeping the corridors clean.

"Wipe your feet!"

And here, someone's hurled his last snowball at the crowd around the entrance. It was a well-shaped, solidly packed snowball. Was it a nervous hand, an inaccurate eye or a hidden

61

desire for revenge which caused the snowball to go off its course—and not we but the window got it.

When I'll be big again, I'll stir up this problem loudly and forcibly; I'll make it the first order of the day. How many windows are we allowed to break in a year? You say, not a single one? That's absurd! You don't believe that yourself.

Glass was supposedly invented by the Phoenecians. And how is it that after so many hundreds of years nothing more durable was invented? What are those chemists doing? and the physicists in their laboratories? Can it really be that there's nothing else?

Let the windows not break. It's their fault, not ours. Why should we freeze and become lifeless suddenly in the face of a threat. Wait for misfortune? Why should I hide, when I'm not guilty, or run away from the spot where the crime occurred? Why was it that, suddenly, all of us present became suspect?

Why, after only these five minutes, after this, well, six-minute recess, should I be faced with this fearsome look and this cruel question:

"Who did it?"

"Not me."

And though I'm telling the truth, I feel as if I'm lying. It would have been proper to say:

"It was an accident. It wasn't me."

I know that there are signs. The snow on my clothes points to me. I threw snowballs just like everyone else. It's allowed isn't it? Well, isn't it? Maybe it isn't? I'm hurrying to class; I want to be on time; for certain I will be. But do I know really? Maybe I'm really to blame? Why didn't I come at the sound of the first bell? But could you have left the game like that, all at once?

"Not me."

I threw some harmless, permissible snowballs. Some? I don't know how many. Do you count the perfect, whole, geometric ones, or the half and quarter ones which you made on the run?

Then there's always the person, the awful liar, who says:

"I only threw two, there, in that direction."

We're all solidly united in the disaster. We feel that the unluckiest person among us is innocent too—because, the fact is, it was an accident which really broke the window; neither the one who really broke it did it, nor did anyone else, for that matter. That's how we feel at this moment and under the threat of shame you can't say anything more than:

"Not me." And not willingly; only under pressure.

And you answer now really: aren't we allowed to break a single window? And if we are allowed one, then shouldn't it be this one really, and right now, at this moment? I know that you won't answer, because you don't know, you don't understand snow. You don't even want to know; you ignore it.

And so, I'll say this:

A person has only just a few such recesses like this one in his whole lifetime. Sometimes, in the course of a whole winter, there might not even be one. Because it has to be just a little warm, otherwise the snow would be powdery and the snow won't stick. And then, your hands freeze too much. The snow has to be moist to hold. It can't be too warm of course, because the snow would melt then. And it has to fall at night or in the morning, so that they wouldn't have time to sweep it up. And it has to be the first snow and untouched, so that there shouldn't be any pieces of ice in it, or bits of soil. We who know and worship snow, feel all this strongly, in our souls.

We know that you're dissatisfied with us. It happens sometimes that you're right. It's true that we jump on the couch too willingly. You say that the couch is falling apart, that the springs are breaking. Not all at once; not right away. We believe it, but being only ten years old, we couldn't prove it.

You don't allow us to crack nuts in the door. We're breaking the door. This is even funnier. The doors—that's the house. Houses are high, strong—they last hundreds of years. Strange! We've only lived for a short time, and just now we've started to observe things. And you—and the whole earth—are strange. But we aren't accusing you of malice. Iron breaks? Agreed? Clothing tears? Alas!

Windows crack? From the slightest cause. They break—of themselves—it's not us. The earth is hard and immovable. I banged myself against the ground, bumped into a wall, a window, a railing, a cupboard, a table, a corner—it hurts; sometimes it's real painful.

And suddenly the Good Lord covered the ground for us, for the children, with a carpet, like a bird laying a nest of down for its young. There is no green grass in winter and there won't be any for a long time to come. And even if there is some, it's fenced off and it's forbidden to walk on it. But with snow you can do whatever you want.

There are harmful snowballs and there are harmless ones just as it is with rifle bullets—some of which are useful, while others are of such a kind that should be outlawed. There's grape-shot, bombs, and grenades. But for you it's always: snowballs which break windows. That's tough. That's war.

And it isn't even me in this case.

"Then who?"

A shrug of shoulders.

"I don't know."

I really don't know. And even if I do, it's still: "I don't know." It only seems to be that it's he. I'll probably find out later for sure, if I inquire casually, investigate. Of course I'm not absolutely certain that it's he, he alone, that it's no one else.

After all, I was hurrying because it was already after the bell; it was late. I was exhausted and overjoyed and afraid too. It could only have seemed to me so, that I knew.

There were two of them. Certainly one of them did it. Someone's face darted past and disappeared. But maybe it was that third person? Maybe it was some confused snowball? It has to be confirmed—you need time, but the teacher wants to know right now. Besides, let someone else tell—maybe he was standing closer; maybe he saw better.

And we stand for a long time sulking and impatient. And I ask myself, in what rarest instance can it happen to a grownup? I can only think of one.

Once, during a procession in which I took part, a shot suddenly resounded. The police immediately surround us: who fired? I'm not guilty but I know that there's going to be an investigation here, that all the "fors" and "againsts" will be solidly weighed. Our children's affairs are resolved only so-so, on the other hand. Why is this so? Why is it that so often we are punished without being guilty? Why is it allowed to punish a child unjustly and then to regard this as a trifle and not be required to answer to anyone for it?

The lesson in religion passed quickly.

I thought about Joseph whom the Pharaoh threw into prison. Joseph was explaining dreams. It turned out well for Joseph later on, but how difficult it must have been to have been sold by his brothers, accused maliciously, and then to have spent long years in chains in a dark cell. I stood for a short time in the corner, but how much did I suffer! I stood in class, where there are windows and I knew that I would stand only until the bell. Why don't we know what the Egyptian prisons looked like, or how long Joseph suffered? I feel sorry for Joseph. I want to feel as sorry for him as he deserved. But I don't know. Before I wanted to know everything about the Eskimos, now it's Joseph. I have a lot of questions; why is it that grownups don't like our questions? Of course, it happened a long time ago and so, they might not know themselves. Why don't grownups like to admit that they don't know; and yet, they'll look in a book or else, ask someone who knows more. Maybe they don't know, but they can figure it out. It's easier for them.

Long ago they didn't even have any pictures in school. In my own time there weren't any movie pictures. How poor were children's lives without movies! They talked about mountains, oceans, deserts, ancient wars, wild people—and more and more the desire to see everything grew. Today, when you leave the dark hall of a movie theater, a person can at least say: "I was there; I saw."

The murmur of the class stirs me from my thinking. We're again hungry and rested for the twelve cannon shots.

Our backs ache, and right now we really begin to feel it. It must have been a hard snowball. But such a small pain is even pleasant. Like a scar which a father shows to his son. A proud, painless pain, about which you say:

"It's nothing. Nothing at all."

I turn around to look at Janek, whom I hit straight in the forehead. His cap even fell off. He felt my glance at once. He smiled and answered with his eyes:

"I remember. But you just wait; it'll start again right away. I won't forgive you."

I don't know whether we laugh more frequently than grownups do or not. But one thing is certain: their laughter says little while we understand perfectly. Sometimes our laughter says more than our words. A meaningful glance, a meaningful smile. Apparently they know, because they forbid us to turn around and laugh in class.

When I'll be a teacher again, I'll try to reach an understanding with my pupils. So that there shouldn't be the feeling of two opposing camps, so to speak; on one side the class while on the other, the teacher and a few of his pets. I'll strive to be sincere. For example: on such a day of the first snow, I'll suddenly clap my hands during the lesson and say: "Everyone remember what he was thinking just at this very moment. Who's ashamed to tell, let him say that he doesn't want to, so that there shouldn't be any constraint."

It doesn't work out at first. But I'll be trying it frequently—as soon as I notice that the class isn't paying attention.

And one by one:

"What were you thinking? And you?"

If someone says that he was thinking about the lesson, I'll ask:

"You aren't making it up are you?"

If someone laughs and I see that he doesn't want to tell, I'll say:

"Maybe you don't want to say it in front of everyone. Then whisper it in my ear or else, I'll write it down during the recess."

And they say: "And why does the teacher want this?"

"I want to write a book about school," I'll answer. "I want everyone to be convinced that you can't always pay attention during a lesson. Maybe the recesses should be longer in winter, or maybe on nice days pupils tire more quickly. Many people write books about school. And each time something new is introduced, to make it better for the pupil and the teacher. Because, one day, you will finish school and go your way, but we go to school our whole life."

And my pupils are greatly surprised because it never occurred to them at all that teachers go to school too, and spend many hours there. We're all going to suggest things that we'd like to see changed. I'll tell them that teachers suffer most from sore throats and nerves. And why we are nervous.

And after everyone relates honestly what he was thinking about during the lesson, I'll joke:

"Now all those who weren't paying attention will get a zero."

"O-o-o, just look how shrewd the teacher is!"

And I: "It isn't nice to say that the teacher's shrewd."

While they: "And why not?"

And so, I explain. And again: "Maybe I should give zeros to those who were paying attention?"

Some start to yell: "Yes, yes, yes!"
While others: "Why us? We were paying attention!"
"You weren't paying attention though," I'll say.
"Why?"
"Because today's the first day of snow, and you don't even notice it."
"But snow isn't the lesson."
"Then maybe I shouldn't give any zeros today."
"Neither today, nor anytime."
"But it's difficult without zeros."
"But a zero is awful."
"And to give zeros is awful too. A teacher would rather give hundreds."
"Then let him."
"But is that allowed?"
"Of course not..."
And we'll banter this way until the bell.

Just think; how strange it all is! I wanted to be little, and now I'm again thinking what I'll be doing when I'm a grownup. It seems that it's not always the best—neither for children nor for adults. Adults have their cares and worries and children their own.

It could be so that a person could alternate being big and little, like summer and winter, day and night, sleep and wakefulness. If that were so, no one would be surprised. And grownups and children would mutually understand one another.

At recess the play was already quieter. We already decided on sides. The snow was all trampled over, and so snowballs were harder to make. Some tried, but more of us preferred to play at sleds. One boy is in the rear—he's the coachman, while two are in front—the horses. And we form a chain, like a carnival parade, or a fire engine, or an artillery gun.

Everyone has his own idea, but we all race: who has better horses, or a car.

At first there was order, but later, it got all mixed up. They started to run into each other. They made a train wreck. They all fell over and are pushing. There's always a wild one to be found in the group, and then someone has to cry. Either they stepped on someone's hand or else, kicked somebody with their boot. It had a metal tap on it. And they squeezed him so hard that he could hardly breathe.

Not all of us like to play wildly. Not at all. Sometimes we'd rather not play at all than to play with someone wild, someone who pushes, yells, and punches. Because if you poke him jokingly, he'll hit you right away with all his might, to get even. He doesn't regard anything—he pushes, tugs, pulls your clothes. As if he were unconscious. How often does a person feel like playing, but says:

"I don't want to."

Because he's there.

"Either it's him or me."

Let them choose themselves.

Sometimes they're even afraid to say what they really think because that one will start calling names, or pestering, or annoying. It's even better:

"I'm not going to play."

If they figure it out themselves—that's good; if not—then that's too bad. It's regrettable. In the playground you don't know all the wild ones; you can't know the whole school. And so, you rather suffer more than not. And you don't have time to arrange things beforehand. Therefore, if someone's first to start up a game, and everyone likes it, then all follow him. It's as if he gives the signal. And it has to be said that the dopes—that's what we call them—have good intentions; only they don't know how to do anything.

And, in truth, we too piled into one another, as if a street car struck an automobile, or two airplanes collided. But there were only two of us, and then we only banged into each other side-ways. Then we start to chase one another and run away and when some wild trio wants to bump into us, we step aside and stop:

"Go away, we don't want to!"

Two runaway cars were chasing each other throughout the whole recess. Our trio was well-matched. Only one horse banged his head at the moment when we were running away from a speeding car. They came up on our side and we didn't have time to move aside when—Bang!—into the other's head. He didn't even cry, only he didn't want to be a horse anymore.

My button was torn off, but I picked it up and put it in my pocket. It would be sewn on again at home.

Only in one place were we bombarded. We galloped past a volley of snowballs. Who doesn't play games, won't understand any of this. It isn't only important that you run around, but also that something is happening inside you. A card game or even a game of chess—that's only throwing down cards or moving mates. A dance—that's turning round in circles. Only the one who plays or dances knows what really takes place.

Games shouldn't be taken lightly, and they shouldn't be interfered with; nor should you interrupt a game abruptly to assign someone as your partner, someone you don't like. If I'm driving a wagon, I want to have the horses of the same size, not too large and not too small. And they should be frisky, but obedient too, and intelligent. And if I'm a horse, I don't want a stupid coachman or a brutish one. Because I set the pace myself, and I don't want to be tugged, or pushed, or whipped. I feel differently as the horse and differently as the driver. And what do you know? That I snorted, that I'm stamping my feet in place impatiently, or that I yell "h-o-o-o-o!"

Anyway, the most important thing is to run around as much as you can, because there's another hour ahead in class.

I don't know if I should return home with Mundek again today. If you have a regular route home, and you start going together with someone, then you have to go with him every time. But it could be unpleasant too, and then it's hard to break away, unless you quarrel for good or even have a fight.

There are those kind with whom no one wants to walk home from school. These always tag along with someone different. Then there are those kind who prefer to return home alone; but there aren't too many of these. Some like a crowd. But most often it's always a pair, or else a trio; two are friends and the third one simply joins up while the other two look at him surprised. Some are jealous when a third one joins in. These kind aren't very nice; it looks like he bought you for himself.

It isn't nice either when one of the pair wants to continue walking together, while the other one got bored, or chose someone else. Then the other one has to steal out of school so that his partner shouldn't see him. If he's sensitive, he'll understand and go home by himself. But others cause trouble, will reveal secrets, make up lies, and from a supposed friend he'll make the worst enemy.

The one you return home from school with doesn't always have to be your friend. Your own friend can live in such an

entirely different direction that you can't even go a little way
with him—it's in the opposite direction from the very start. And
so, it's an entirely different thing—a friend, or the person with
whom you like to go home after school. A friend is always like a
brother, or even better sometimes. Only you know your brother
better and so you can't make a mistake with him. But when a
person gets close to another one by means of words, it seems
that he's such and such a kind, but you can make a mistake
because he can be false. He's one way to your face and another
behind your back, or else he'll say one thing and do another.
And if your brother doesn't turn out, then there's no hope; you
argue with him but in the end you have to make up. But with a
supposed friend, you can separate for good.

When I was little for the first time, I also had many different
friends. The first one lasted a whole year, but I only liked him
for a few months. I saw that he tried to talk me into getting into
trouble. And so, I waited for him to break off our friendship, to
go his own way. But he wouldn't. Until he got left behind in
class. That's how I got free of him.

The second friendship didn't turn out well either. But it was
easy to quarrel with him. I gave him a few presents, loaned him fifty
or sixty cents (and that way I purchased my way free of him).

Long afterwards, I was very careful. Others tried to make
friends with me. I would go with them once, twice, but then I
made it appear that I had to go somewhere or that I forgot my
pen and had to return to school, or else, before the bell, I would
get all my things ready and then, in the rush, I'd grab my coat
and rush off.

"What happened to you yesterday? I waited for you."

"I don't know. I went home by myself."

Until I found a friend. A real friend. The kind who, when he
doesn't show up in school, makes you feel sad. I want to sit with
him in class. And in the recess I won't play without him. But he
often omitted the recess—then more and more. We didn't horse
around on the street, because he walked slowly.

The others talked:

"Doesn't it bore you, the way he plods on. He's a sissy. And
he kisses girls too."

He wasn't a sissy at all. Only he had a heart disease. And
he didn't kiss girls at all. He had a cousin. We were already big—

in the fourth or fifth grade, while she was in the first. And some-times we met her and she used to kiss him. She was little, and she was his aunt's daughter besides. What's wrong with that?

I also had another friend. He was two grades higher than me. Sometimes it happens that an older boy will get acquainted with a smaller one and they walk home together if it happens that their classes are let out at the same time. But once he told me to wait for him and later walked with his friend and was talking to him pretending that he didn't see me. I'm ambling along on the side like a wagon's fifth wheel. I see that he's busy and so I cross over to the other side of the street and look to see if he's going to ask why I'm leaving. But he doesn't say anything. I wasn't offended, but I thought: "He's doing me a fa-vor." And that's how it ended.

I remember everything and now I'm careful. I prefer to wait until I find someone with whom I can not only run around with but also someone with whom I can talk about different things. Not only about school, but about things in general.

And so, I'm walking home and Mundek catches up with me. "I was looking for you in school." he said.

I don't answer anything. We walk side by side and he asks: "Maybe you don't feel like walking with me?"

I see that he's sensitive. Another wouldn't ask.

"Sure I do," I say.

He glances at me carefully, to see whether I really meant it, or whether I said it just for the sake of answering. We burst out laughing.

"You want to chase a trolley?"

"We do that every day. I ran around enough during the recesses."

We stopped in front of a store window.

"Sa-a-y, look! Aren't those neat compasses. See, that's what you insert if you want to make a big circle. What do you think, how much can such compasses cost? Would you like to have one? Look here, gold ink. And what a tiny ink-bottle; for travel-ling. I have to buy a brush, but not here. Frankowski bought one on the corner and he has it a month already. The hairs fell out of mine right away. The robbers! If you could, what would you pick from the window? If they'd let you have one thing? I'd choose a compass, and this little black doll."

71

"But that's two things."

"Well, the compass then."

In the shop next door, we choose a big bar of chocolate, just in case they'd let us. Later on, Mundek selected a vase for his mother, while I chose a doll for little Irene. The jeweler's display has watches together with rings and brooches with precious stones in them. We aren't greedy. We're interested in the watches. We deliberated a long time—whether a wrist watch is better or a pocket watch on a chain.

We children are different from you grownups. The market price of an item interests us but little. We only know the things which are useful and not useful and we're always ready to trade something expensive but unnecessary for something we feel we have to have. If you wanted to learn the secret of our business transactions, you would have to know that a deal between us, otherwise looks like a swindle.

When I was little for the first time, I got a pair of ice-skates as a present. At that time, ice-skates were still a rare thing, a rare present, an expensive one. Well, I exchanged the skates for a pen-case made of cherry wood. It was round and had a little toy dog attached to it. The dog was missing one eye but it was very nice. You need a pen-box every day, but the ice-skates you use rarely. And the winter happened to be mild; there was no ice. When they found out at home what I did, they made a real scene. I had to give back the case. It was very embarrassing because if the skates were really mine, I should have had the right to do whatever I pleased with them. What does it matter to anyone that I preferred a pen-case made of a fragrant wood and with a blind dog on it? He wasn't cheating me at all, that other boy. I knew that the skates were more expensive, but I wanted to have the pen-case. And wouldn't a traveller in the desert give away a sack of precious pearls for a pitcher of water?

We advised one another for a long time about what to select from the cabinet maker's window. We both wanted to have a little table that had a drawer with a lock on it; but would they let us put it in our room? Or maybe something for our parents? But it would be very nice to have at least a small table, all one's own.

We started to talk about our homes; that it's awful for him because his father drinks.

It's a terrible thing to have a drunkard for a father. They shouldn't allow drunkards to marry. Because, afterwards, the wife and children only suffer.

"We're afraid each pay-day: will father bring home the money or will we be hungry all week? And just think how awful it is: when he's drunk he doesn't know what's happening to him, but after he sleeps it off he feels ashamed and his head hurts."

"Can't you tell him to stop?"

"What can I say? Mama cries enough and yells and swears. He promises, but it's always the same. He's like a child."

"But why don't you try to tell him sincerely?"

"I'm ashamed somehow. Once we were visiting Papa's friend in the country. They were drinking there, but Papa said that he didn't want to. He had just sworn to Mama that he wouldn't take any drink to his lips. And so they began to talk him into it, to have him try at least one little glass. I tugged at Papa's sleeve because I knew that if he had one glass, then he would have others. At this Papa got up and said: "Let's go down to the river." And we went. Birds were singing. And it seemed that the wheat was bowing to us. The sun was shining. It was really nice and pleasant. Papa is holding me by the hand. We sat down near the river and Papa is still holding my hand. And his hand quivered once, as if he were stung by a nettle. I said, "You see, Papa, it's better not to drink." He glanced at

73

me and I got terribly embarrassed and I felt very sorry for him. Because he looked at me so sadly. You know, sometimes a dog will look at you that way when he's begging for something, or when he's afraid that you're going to beat him. I know. I know it's one thing with a person and another thing with a dog. But that's how it seemed to me. For the life of me I wouldn't ever say such a thing to Papa again. Well, you see: it was as if he came to a conclusion, staring at the water all the while and finally saying: "It's a dog's life, sonny." And he sighed. I feel like kissing his hand, to apologize. But Papa is holding my hand firmly and doesn't let go. I really don't know if he was offended by my words; maybe he thought that he was unworthy to be kissed. Papa didn't return to the others, only he asked me to bring him his walking stick and to tell them that he had a headache. He didn't want them to laugh at him. In a shop he bought some cracknels. I didn't eat a single one of them. I gave them all to my little brother. I really wanted to eat a couple of them so that Papa wouldn't think that I was scorning him. But I just couldn't. Something was choking me. He didn't drink afterwards for a long time, a month maybe, and Mama thought that was good. Then someone told Mama that when a person is trying to break his habit and he walks around downcast and dejected, it means that he hasn't broken it yet; only when he stops thinking about it and is again gay and happy does it mean that he won't do it anymore. Only listen: don't tell anyone is school. I'm only telling you this. You won't tell, will you? Even if we should quarrel?"

"Why should we quarrel?"

"Don't you know? Something'll come up and we'll have a fight."

And we talked a little more about something, about the kinds of people there are in the world: one drinks, another doesn't want to work, a third steals, one likes one thing, another another. Either he likes it or he doesn't. For example: there are people who don't like to trim their finger-nails. Because it hurts. And then they have long nails. Or else, they bite them. Or that you get splinters in your fingers and they hurt. Or else, you can get white spots on your finger-nails; what's the reason?

They say it's a sign of good-luck. But others say that someone's jealous. It's always this way; everyone says something else and in the end you don't know whom to believe. There's an awful lot of lying in the world.

We talked this way for such a long time that I was late for lunch. I walked him home first, and then he walked me and so, we walked back and forth. It was pleasant though, to walk and talk, because there's snow everywhere.

Mama begins to complain about why I was late for lunch; that I was running around; that she has enough of cooking and washing dishes; that I'm wearing out my shoes; that I'm not a girl, otherwise I would help out; that she'll go to school and complain; that I'll grow up to be a lazy good-for-nothing; that Irene ought to be older and I younger; that she'll die because of me.

I'm standing, listening, but I don't understand a thing.

If I was late, then I can eat a cold lunch, or not eat at all; and I can wash my own dish too.

Mama brought me my lunch, but I don't feel like eating. She begins to yell even louder:

"Here. Now eat! He's going to complain yet, and make faces."

I don't want to annoy Mama any further and so I eat. But every biteful sticks in my throat. I can't swallow. I say a prayer so that the food might disappear suddenly.

It was only in the evening that I learned that the moths ate holes in Mama's dress. There's going to be a name-day party, and the moths ruined her dress. And so, children have to suffer because of what the moths did.

The injustice hurt me even more. It's better even not to know the reason why grownups are angry or, when they scold you. You sense that something happened to them, but you look for the blame in yourself, too. Until you find it.

I sat down in my little corner and am doing my lessons. But I'm afraid that one of my friends will come and then it will all start over again:

"Go, tear your shoes; your boy-friends are calling you already."

But really, that's why I wanted to be little again, to be able to play with my friends again.

I guessed correctly, because someone knocked very softly on the door, and once only. But Mama heard: "Don't even think about going out. Do your homework."

I continue my lessons. I don't even feel like going out anymore.

And I imagine that I'm sitting alone in a field, and it's night and cold, and I'm all alone, barefoot and hungry. And there are wolves howling all around me. I'm cold and afraid. I'm shivering all over.

Man is strange. Either he's happy or else, suddenly, he's sad.

I'm not absolutely certain, but it seems to me that grownups are angry more than they are sad. Or it may be that inside they're sad and they pity themselves when they're angry at children. Rarely do we say about a teacher;

"You were sad today, Sir."

But unfortunately and more frequently we say:

"The teacher was angry."

Children cry more often than grownups do, and not because they're cry-babies, but because they are more sensitive, because they suffer more.

Why don't grownups respect our children's tears? It seems to them that we cry over everything and anything. That's not true though. Little children cry because it's their only defense: he makes a big fuss; someone'll be found who will take notice and come to help. Or else, he'll cry from despair. While we rarely cry, and not always about the most important things. If something hurts us really, then we might shed one tear and that's the end of it. And it happens with grownups that when there's a misfortune, his tears will dry up suddenly and grow cold.

You cry the least when they're angry about something and are wrong. You'll just lower your head and nothing more. Sometimes they question you, but you don't answer. Sometimes you want to answer but all you can do is to move your lips—you can't. They call it stubbornness. And sometimes some kind of obstinacy takes hold of you and you think that nothing matters; let them give you a beating; it will end anyway. And so, you'll raise your arm or else, whisper something under your nose. Because the worst kinds of words and thoughts are buzzing around inside your head. That's when you lose control over yourself and no matter whether it's the teacher or your own father. Or, on the other hand, there's nothing going on in your head, but in your breast you feel anger and misery.

Often you don't even hear them yelling, or else, you don't understand a single word. You don't even know what they're upset about. Only your eyes are swimming and your head's buzzing.

And they shake you yet, and push and hit. They hit you once or else yank you by the arm and it seems to them that it doesn't hurt. They call hitting children punishment. When they're beating a child with a strap, they hold him and wallop him like a criminal while the child's struggling and yelling:

"I won't anymore, I won't anymore."

For such a beating—maybe it's rare nowadays, but it still exists—they'll take you to court in the future. What does he feel, the one who gives the beating, or the one who's getting it? I don't know. But we look upon it with disgust, indignation, and horror. We seem to take more pity on a horse than adults do on a person.

Maybe you think that, among ourselves, we also fight this way? But we have small hands and we aren't very strong. And even in the greatest anger we don't fight so viciously. You don't know our fights. We always try, ahead of time, to see who's stronger, and we size up the strength according to age and resistance. He sizes me up, and I him. And if it happens that one of us is pinned down, is unable to move any more, then we stop at once. Or, if it happens that someone's butting in, then we might punch too hard. Or when we're pushing one another, you can get punched in the nose, and it can bleed.

We know what it means—it hurts.

(Some doctor in a mental institution reported that children in penal homes are less sensitive. I would have measured his own sensitivity and given him fifty lashes. It's a disgrace that a scientist can write such a thing.)

I'm sitting this way contemplating what I knew before and what I now know. And more and more am I overcome by a feeling of regret that we are so small and weak. And mostly I'm sorry for Mundek, because his father is a drunkard.

And so, I'll probably be his friend. He's not too well off, and neither am I. Let there be friendship then between us. And I'm suffering right now because of him, because it was his fault that I was late for lunch.

My eyes grew warm suddenly, and I quickly pushed my pad aside to keep it from getting wet. But no: the tears flowed into my nose; they didn't fall.

And here comes little Irene up to me. She is standing at a distance from me, and is watching. I look at her from the corner of my eye, because I don't know what she wants. She's standing quietly at first, and then she takes a step closer; but still she doesn't say anything. She just stands there. I'm waiting while she's holding something and is passing it from one hand to the other. I know that something good will come out of all this and, slowly, I'm overcome by tenderness. I grow calm. And then Irene stretches her hand out and hands me something. She wants to make me a present of a piece of ground glass. When you look through it, everything appears in different colors. Yesterday I asked her for it and she didn't even let me have a look through it. But now she says:

"Here, for always."

I don't know whether she said "take it" or not, because I didn't hear. I only heard "for always;" she said it so quietly, so gently and sweetly.

I didn't want to take it. Later, we might quarrel or else she'll regret it and will then want it back. And she'll complain yet that I took it myself. It's hard to reach an understanding with little children, because grownups interfere. When they make fun and laugh at us that we're so small, then we...we feel even smaller. Why, a child will say sincerely, "for always," and here we poke fun at him. And so, I didn't want to take it, because I didn't trust her. I'm afraid that I'll suffer afterwards. But I took it finally, and looking through it, I see, instead of one lens, many windows—of different colors.

"I'll give it back," I say.

"You don't have to," she answers.

And then, she put her tiny hand on top of my large hand. I look at her hand through the lens—and we burst out laughing together.

But, here, Mama is asking whether I finished my homework. She tells me that she's going to give me trolley fare so that I could take the dress which the moths ate to my aunt. I think to myself:

"Good, at least this will get me out of the house for a little while."

"Only don't lose it," Mama says.

But I only thought to myself: "A girl might lose it, but not me."

Because when they complain that we're boys, they themselves only cause us to pick on girls. And are we to blame? That's how we were born!

And its always: "Boys, boys!" while we answer in revenge: "Girls are so and so." As if there were two enemy camps. We know ourselves our own worth and theirs too.

78

I take the dress which Mama already wrapped up and am leaving.

I have to wait for a long time for the street-car and I'm angry because I wanted to return in a flash, to show them how fast I could do it. But something happened somewhere and the street-cars were held up. And when the street-car did come finally, it was already full. But the people pushed anyway, and I did too. I'm already holding onto the handle, to get on, when, here, someone gave me such a hard shove that I was knocked off. I was so angry that I yelled. But he's standing on the step and says:

"Where are you crawling? You'll fall off!"

"You're real considerate," I thought, "you'll fall off yourself, you drunkard." He wasn't drunk at all, only I was so angry. He was fully sober when he pushed me off the street-car, and he was big and strong.

I wait some more. The second trolley is full too. I paid my fare and am on my way. But I'm thinking all the while how rudely that man pushed me off. Such a boor, a brute, and a grownup too—he's setting an example.

And again someone shoved me. He kind of raked me aside, as if I weren't alive; I almost lost my package. And what was so wrong in what I said to him? Anyone would have said the same:

"Careful."

And he all but sat on me:

"I'll give you 'careful'!"

I repeated it: "So, be more careful."

And he grabbed me by the chin.

"Let go of me," I say.

"Don't complain then."

And here, some old man butts in. He didn't see anything, doesn't know anything, but he starts:

"That's how they're brought up nowadays! The scamp won't make way for an older person."

"Because he didn't ask me to make way," I answer.

And the first one continues: "Let me tell you, you young pup!"

"I'm not a pup, but a person. And you had no right to push me."

"Are you going to give me a lesson, tell me what right I have?"

"You bet."

My heart is pounding and my throat feels like it's choking. Let there be a scene. I won't give in. And here, people are beginning to take notice. They're surprised that such a little person is biting back so.

"And what will you do if I pull your ears," he says.

"I'll call a policeman and I'll tell him to arrest you for creating a scene in the trolley."

If everyone didn't start laughing at this moment! And he too. They're not even angry anymore; they're only laughing as if I told some joke. They're even getting up from their seats to have a look at me. I can't stand it any longer, so I say:

"Excuse me, but I want to get off now."

But he restrains me. "You just got on," he says. "Take a little ride for yourself."

And a fat woman is sitting to one side, sprawling all over the seat interferes:

"What a nasty child!"

I didn't hear their barbs any more.

"I want to get off," I shout

But he doesn't budge. "You'll make it," he says, "you're young. What's your hurry?"

I yelled with all my strength: "Conductor!"

Finally, someone interceded" "Let him go there now!"

I got off and everyone is looking at me as if at some strange creature. They probably laughed for half an hour afterwards.

They tell us to respect them. But I wonder what for? They're rude. The Commandment teaches: "Honor your father," but not every grownup. That requires some skill. And what should Mundek do if he has a drunkard for a father? "Young pup, scamp, bad upbringing." Then give a good example yourself of a good upbringing! And how about the teacher who was picking his nose for a whole hour during the lesson? Why should he restrain himself in front of young pups? And they call us scamps yet. Just to offend and humiliate. Is it so strange then that when children grow up themselves, they go about in the world so enraged?

We are conscious; we see and know a lot; we feel and guess a lot more. Only we have to pretend, because they've sealed our lips. One teacher picks his nose during the lesson, another turns to the window, secretly takes out her mirror, and paints her lips. Do they think that we're blind, when there are forty of us sitting there? Why don't they behave that way when the principal visits?

And they're surprised when, sometimes, you do something to them out of spite. After all, we feel that they're doing us a harm. They have morals only on their tongues, while they instill in us falsehood and servility. So that, when we grow up, we'll push aside the weak and cringe before the strong.

I'm walking with the package under my arm while in my mind grownup thoughts are getting tangled with a child's suffering and offense. I only went four stops beyond, but it's still a long way to my aunt's. But I prefer to run at full speed rather than to bicker with them.

And at home, Mama asks annoyed: "Where were you sitting so long?"

I didn't answer anything. Only it seemed to me suddenly that it was Mama who was to blame for everything. If I didn't leave the house already upset, then maybe I wouldn't have created a scene on the trolley. You give in so many times, then why not once more. And that proverb, like a joke, says that a wise person makes way for the fool. Now look around for the wise person!

I regret that the day, which began so beautifully, ended so badly.

I'm lying in bed now, but I don't sleep. I'm thinking: "I guess this is how it has to be. It isn't so ideal at home, but it's even worse somewhere else in the world. Did it seem so amusing to them then? Because I'm small I'm not allowed to call a policeman? That they have the right to push me out of the trolley, pull me by the chin, and threaten me with a beating."

Aren't children people after all? Or aren't they? And now I don't know myself whether to be glad that I'm a child again, that the snow is white again; or to be sad because I'm weak.

Until thoughts come to my rescue. Because no matter how many times life seems difficult, there is always at least a measure of comfort to be gotten from some thought. It begins this way: "Oh, how good it would be if..." and more and more until it seems that it's all happening.

"And so, it seems that I'm still a child, but I have the strength of a grownup, a Mr. Atlas. I'm a strong-man. And when he told me on the trolley that he's going to pull my ears, I say: "If you please." And when I squeeze his hand, he almost jumps from the pain. "Let me go," he cries. But I say: "Why, you were going to pull my ears. If I'm such a little pup, then why don't you go ahead and pull them?" And I squeeze his hand still harder. He brings his other hand up, but I grab it. "Let me go! Let me go this instant!" "When you apologize, I will."

It was fun to imagine this and make believe. And since I was holding the package in one hand, I couldn't hold him with it at the same time.

Grownups think it's strange that boys want to be strong. And is a lion stronger than a bear? And can the strongest man defend himself when a hundred others jump on him? And is the trolley-car conductor stronger or is the gym teacher? Who's the strongest one in the class? in the whole school? in the whole country? Who will pin whom down? who can go farther, higher—run, throw, or jump?

It isn't a child's silly curiosity, nor is it a game, but a test—against whom can we manage to defend ourselves.

Grownups don't know how much a small boy suffers at the hands of an older and stronger one. He'll grab something out of your hand and run off, or he'll hit you and laugh yet, because he knows that you won't do anything to him; he'll push your cap off your head, spoil your game, won't let you watch. And you can't do anything. Unless you throw yourself at him like a madman. And he'll beat you up yet. It's always easier for him to break free from your hold, because he's stronger. And you don't always tell on him because they don't help you at all while he'll only want to get even with you. Those kind can do with us whatever they want.

If you happen to be quick and agile, you even shout something to him, or hit him, and then run away.

There is no law or justice among us. We live like prehistoric people. There are those who attack and those who hide and run away. And there's the fist and the stick and the stone too. There's neither organization nor civilization. There may seem to be, but only for grownups, not for children.

Our speech is meager and awkward (at least it seems to you this way, because it's ungrammatical). That's why it seems to you that we think little and feel even less. Our beliefs are naive because we have no book knowledge, while the world is so big. Tradition replaces the written law. You don't understand our ways, and you have no insight into our affairs.

We live like a race of little people subjugated by a race of big people which possesses physical strength and secret knowledge.

We are an oppressed class which you want to keep alive only at the price of the smallest self-denial, the least effort to you.

We are exceedingly complicated beings. In addition we are taciturn, suspicious, and reticent and your crystal balls won't tell you a thing unless you have faith in us, and feeling for us.

An ethnologist ought to study us, or a sociologist, or a naturalist, but not a pedagogue or a demagogue.

Our only friend among you is the artist who is generous to us in the moment of his inspiration, that rare and capricious and exceptional moment. At that time he reminds you that there are children. But he, too, will only tell you a fairy-tale.

Very well then: you behave towards us with humor—rarely kindly and often with anger.

I awoke feeling sad.

Patch

I awoke feeling sad.

It isn't too bad when a person feels sad. Sadness—that's a gentle and pleasant thing. Good thoughts come into your head then. You feel sorry for everybody; for Mama, that the moths ate holes in her dress; for Papa, that he has to work hard; and for Grandma, that she's old and will die soon; and for my dog, that he's cold; and for the flower, because its leaves wilted and maybe it's sick. You want to help everybody and you want to improve yourself.

Isn't it true that we like sad tales? That must mean that we need sadness too sometimes. Sadness is like an angel who stands near by and watches over you and who places his hand on your head and sighs with his wings.

A person would like to be alone or else with another person, to talk over different things with.

And he's afraid lest someone should spoil this sadness—not exactly spoil, but rather, frighten it away.

I stood by the window and on the panes of glass pretty flowers formed during the night. Maybe they looked more like leaves than flowers—kind of like palms. Strange leaves, a strange world. Because, how did they get that way, from where?

"Why aren't you getting dressed?" Papa asks.

I don't answer, only I walk up to him and say: "Good morning." I kissed his hand too, and he glanced at me. Now I dress quickly. Then I eat breakfast and am off to school.

"Why are you rushing off so?" Mama asks.

"I'll stop into church," I say.

Because I remembered that I don't pray very much, and I felt badly.

And so, I step outside and look to see if Mundek is coming. But he isn't. The water froze everywhere. Some boys already started a slide—to have it real smooth. At first it's only a little piece, but it grows slowly. In the end it's so big that everybody can slide on it.

I stopped near it, but I don't try it. I walk on.

And instead of Mundek, I meet Wisniewski. And he says: "Hey there, tripshtick, how are you?"

At first I didn't know what he wanted. Then I remembered—he was giving me a new nick-name. Because of that drawing I made—because I drew a triptych.

"Go away," I answer.

And he comes to attention, salutes and says: "An order, Sir."

I see that he's trying to start something, and therefore I cross over to the other side of the street. He even gave me a shove as I went past, and so I turned into a side street.

"I have time," I think to myself. "I'll make a detour."

I walk to school reluctantly. It's noisy there, and everybody's pushing or saying something. Sometimes, I walk slowly on purpose or else, I take the long way to get to school just when the lessons begin. It's pleasant to arrive exactly at the bell, because the teacher enters immediately and it becomes quiet. If you had a watch, you could time it perfectly. But this way, you can be late.

It doesn't matter. I turned into still another street—as if someone were calling me there, or prodding me. It happens that a person does something and he doesn't even know himself why he does it. And it turns out either good or bad. If it turns out bad, then you say that you were tempted. Because it's only afterwards that you are surprised: why did I do that?

And so, I don't know myself, but I go more and more out of my way. I'm walking and here, all of a sudden on the snow, there's a little dog. Such a little dog. Such a little dog, and so scared. He's standing on three legs while holding the fourth in the air. And he's shivering and shaking. The street is empty. Only in the distance is someone to be seen moving.

I'm standing and looking at him and I'm thinking that they probably chased him out of the house and he doesn't know where to go. He's all white except for one ear and the tip of his tail, which are jet black. His paw is hanging in the air so, and he's looking at me sorrowfully. He wants me to take care of him. He even raised his tail and wagged it twice somehow, sadly—one way and then the other, as if hope entered him. Then he starts towards me, but it's clear that his foot hurts. That's how it seemed to me. And again he's standing and waiting. And that one black ear of his is raised while the white one is hanging. It looked exactly as if he were begging, but is still afraid. He licked his nose with his tongue—he's probably hungry—and is looking at me meekly.

I take a few steps to see what he would do. And he follows me. He limps on his three legs and each time I turn around, he stops. It occurred to me to stamp my foot and shout, "Go home!" to see where he'd go. But I felt sorry for him. I don't shout but only say: "Go home, or you'll freeze."

And here, suddenly, he runs straight to me. What can I do? I can't leave him here; he'll freeze surely. He came up to me very close, crouched down to the ground, and is shivering all over. And I'm certain now, absolutely certain, that my little Patch is homeless. Maybe he was roaming around all night? Maybe this was his last hour? And I was going to school by an entirely different route. I can be just the person to save him in this last hour.

I pick him up in my arms and he licked me. He's cold all over and only his tongue is a little warm. And so, I quickly unbutton my coat and put him inside—only his head is poking out, just enough for him to breathe. He scratched with his paws until he caught onto something so as not to fall out. I want to hold him up, but I'm afraid I might hurt his paw. Therefore, I put my arm around him and I could feel his heart beating. It's beating so fast that it feels like it's pounding.

If I knew that Mama would let me keep him, I could still make it back home. What harm would there be if I had him? I would feed him from my own food. But I'm afraid to return home and they won't let me in school with him. And here, he's gotten comfortable under my coat and he stopped moving about. He closed his eyes and I hold him this way under my coat. My sleeve was pulled up a little and he doesn't even want to breathe the cold air. Only he shoved his muzzle into my sleeve and is panting. His whole body now begins to get warm. He'll probably fall asleep now. And then that will I do?

I look around and see a little shop. "What will be, will be," I think. "I'll go in. Maybe it got lost from this shop. I'll ask." I know that it isn't, but I try. What else could I do? And so, I enter and ask:

"Is this your dog, Ma'am?"

She looks at me and says: "No." But I don't leave right away. If I had some money I'd buy him some milk. But the lady asks: "Let me see him." I unbutton my coat quickly and take him out. "O-o-o," I say, "He's asleep." And the woman, as if having thought of something, again says: "No, he's not mine."

"But maybe you know whose dog he is?" I ask, "He has to be from around here."

"I don't know," she says.

"But he's cold, Ma'am."

And I'm holding him in such a way that he doesn't even stir—he's sleeping so hard. If I didn't feel heart, I would think that he was dead.

I'm ashamed to ask her to keep him for me in the meantime, until I return. But it occurred to me that maybe the janitor would hold him for me, if she wouldn't. The janitor on the first floor isn't nice. He's not like the one on the second floor. That one talks to us, and jokes and even sharpens our pencils for us.

But here, the woman asks: "You live on this street?" She pretends that she doesn't know me, that I don't buy anything in her shop—and so, why am I standing there?

"Well, go now, go," she says, "Your mother sent you to school and you're playing with a dog. And close the door tightly."

She probably thought that I was so wrapped up in my thoughts that I'd forget to close the door behind me, and that I'd let in the cold. Everyone thinks only that it should be warm for him. But a dog is God's creature too.

I'm leaving, but I really don't know what to do. And so, I try again:

"But look Ma'am, he's so white. He isn't mangy at all." And I shield his lame paw. Maybe it's only frostbitten?

"Don't bother me with that dog now."

There you have it: I'm bothering her. As if it's my fault that the dog is freezing out in the cold.

Well, it's too bad. If the janitor doesn't agree to it, then let him put the dog out himself. And the children will make a big commotion in school right away.

"O-o-oh! A dog—he brought a dog!"

And then, some teacher will find out. It has to be kept a secret. But I've already lost so much time unnecessarily, and so, I stuff him back—this time under my jacket. I don't even pay attention to the fact that it may be stuffy for him there.

And I'm running to school now. The janitor will probably agree to it. And I'll borrow a few pennies from someone and buy some milk for my little Patch.

I named him Patch.

I'm running this way with him, and he's gotten completely warm. He awoke and started scratching and twisting until his nose poked out and he barked out, rather, growled. By the sound of his voice, it seemed to me that he felt good and that he was thanking me. At first, I could feel his cold body against my chest, but now, he was warming me. As if I were fondling a baby. And he blinked his eyes.

I went straight to the janitor: "Please Sir, could you hide him for me? He was so frozen."

"Who's frozen?"

"He is."

He saw that I was holding a dog and he became annoyed.

"And where did you find him?"

"On the street."

"Why did you take him, somebody else's dog?"

"He doesn't have a home; he's an orphan. His paw is hurt."

"And where am I going to hide him? Why did you bring him? Maybe he belonged to someone there?"

"No one," I say. "I asked everyone whose dog it was—they wouldn't have chased him out into the cold."

"Maybe he's dirty," he says.

"What are you saying! He's all white." As if I got offended. But I'm glad, because he takes him to look him over. Maybe he'll keep him. But here, a boy spots him, and so I quickly shove him under my coat. And the janitor tells the boy: "Go away. Look, you got snow all over your boots." And he chased him away. But he still doesn't want to take him. He says: "There are so many of you here. If everyone starts bringing me a dog from the streets?"

"Please, Sir. Just for a few hours. I'll take him right home."

"They'll let you keep him?"

"I'll go home by the same street. Maybe someone will claim him."

He scratched his forehead and I think to myself: "It's all right."

But he still hesitates. "I have enough with you boys," he says, "and dogs yet."

But he took him in the end. He's a good person. That one from the first floor wouldn't have taken him; he would even have suspected something.

The janitor took him. And some boys already began to gather around. And my Patch seems to understand. He isn't shivering anymore. He's looking at me. And then the bell rang. I left Patch there and made it to class on time. The lesson began.

I'm sitting, but I feel sad. Patch is probably safe now, but he must be hungry. I'm sitting, thinking, wondering where I'm going to get some money to be able to buy Patch some milk.

I'm sitting and I'm thinking that I slept the whole night in a warm bed and didn't know at all that the dog was spending the night out in the cold. And even if I knew, I couldn't have done anything anyway. Well! I wasn't going to get dressed and go out looking for Patch in the streets?

I'm sitting, feeling sad. I could share my sadness with the whole class. I'll probably never run around with the boys again. Yesterday we played at horses and hunting. Such childish games. They're of no use to anyone. If they would let me keep my dog at home, then, at least, I would take care of him. I'd give him a bath, brush his fur; he'd have to be as white as snow. If he wanted, I could teach him different tricks. I'd be patient with him; I wouldn't beat him. I wouldn't even scold him. Because a word hurts as much as a blow.

If you happen to like a teacher, then even the slightest remark hurts. He'll say: "Don't turn around so" or "Don't talk," or "You're not paying attention." And you already feel hurt. You look at him right away to see whether he said it just for the sake of saying it, or whether he's really angry.

And Patch will like me. If he makes a trick wrong—well, I'll tell him it was wrong, but I'll pet him right away, and he'll wag his tail and try harder. I won't tease him, not even for fun, because I don't want to teach him to be angry. It's strange why it should be fun to tease a dog, make him bark. And yesterday I frightened a cat. His heart probably beat real hard out of fright. And are cats really deceitful, or do they just say that?

And the teacher says: "Read further."

As if to me. But I don't know what's going on because I didn't even open my book. I'm standing like a fool. I'm gaping at her and I feel sorry for Patch and for myself. Then Wisniewski says: "Trypshtyck was day-dreaming." My eyes got filled with tears and so, I quickly lowered my head—I didn't want anyone to see. The teacher wasn't angry though. She just said:

"You didn't even open your book. I'll probably have to put you outside the door."

She said "put" and not "throw out." And she didn't even throw me out, only:

"Stand by your desk."

And not even in the corner.

She had to guess that something had happened. Because, if I were a teacher and a pupil was sitting over an unopened book, I would ask what was troubling him, what was the matter with him.

And if my teacher asked me why I wasn't paying attention, would I have told her? Of course not. Of what interest could it be to her? A lesson's a lesson. And I wouldn't betray the janitor either.

"Stand by your desk."

And then she adds: "But maybe you'd prefer it behind the door?"

I blush so hard that I can't answer anything. But all the others get excited. "Yes, behind the door," some say, while others: "He doesn't want to, teacher."

The slightest pretext and they make a joke of it, satisfied that the lesson's been interrupted. They don't think that maybe it's awkward for a person, or that they'll make the teacher angry.

But here, the bell rang and that's how it all ended. And then I'm running to the janitor.

But the janitor from my floor stops me—the angry one.

"Where are you going?" he asks. "Don't you know you can't?"

I'm already afraid, but I think:

"I'll borrow ten cents from someone for the milk."

Maybe from Backiewicz. He always has money. No, he won't loan me any. I hardly know him. Once, when they tried to borrow from him, he said:

"I should loan you money yet, you crook."

I think: "Maybe he will, or maybe someone else," and I look around. And then I remember that Frankowski owes me five cents. I look for him, but he's playing—he's avoiding me.

"Listen. Let me have the five cents back."

"Go 'way," he says, "Don't bother me."

"But I need it."

"Later, I can't now."

"But I need it!"

"I'm telling you, later! I don't have it now."

I see that he's starting to get mad, and that he doesn't have it. So what could I do. I go to Backiewicz. His father has a store, he's rich.

"Why do you want it?" he asks.

"I really need it for something."

"And when will you pay me back?"

"When I have it."

What else could I say. Another would say: "Tomorrow." But he doesn't do anything about it. He even complains when you remind him. "Leave me alone," he'll say.

Grownups, even the poorest ones, have at least twelve cents, while we have to endure all sorts of things for a mere five cents. We suffer a lot because of this, that we don't possess even the smallest amount. And not just once, but continually. If you could only know in advance that you would have them.

"Well, are you going to loan it to me?"

"But I don't have any."

"You do," I say, "but you don't want to give me any."

Had I told him what I wanted it for, he probably would have loaned it to me. Then maybe I should tell him?

While he: "I already loaned out a lot, and no one wants to pay me back. Why don't you go to Frank. He owes me a quarter for over a month now."

But Frank never returns what he borrows. And so, I grimaced. I have no choice.

I can't find Frank though. And then, where am I going to look for him in such a crowd. Backiewicz is even good-hearted, because he doesn't like to refuse. But he's very nosy too: he wants to know everything. He comes up to me himself:

"Well, did he give it to you?"

"I don't know where he is."

He thought for a brief moment and then said:

"Tell me now, why do you need it?"

"Then will you give it to me?"

"Yes, I will."

"Do you have it, though?"

"I have, but I want to buy a piece of ply-wood. I want to make a frame."

And so, I told him quickly and then we're both sneaking up to the second floor when the bell rings. We have to go to class.

I'm uneasy. Patch is hungry; maybe he'll start to bark and whine and the janitor will take him and throw him out.

I named him Patch. But now, I don't think it's so good. It sounds too much like a nick-name. A dog doesn't understand, but it would be awkward for a person. Maybe I'll call him Whitey because I found him in the snow? Or else, Frost or Frosty. Or something about winter.

I'm already thinking as if I know that they'll let me keep him.

But the woman in the shop and the janitor told me that he as an owner. And one could question the boys who live near that gate. But there wasn't even a gate near the place where he was found! And then, what if someone claims him even if it isn't so: he'll play with him a little and then throw him out on the snow again. And even if it's really so, they must not care for him anyway—they already threw him out once. But maybe he ran away himself? I don't even know what he's like. Pups are mischievous. Maybe he did something wrong, was afraid to get punished, and so ran out of the house.

I'm troubled because I don't know what to do. Because it's this and this and this—as if I had a baby, I'm so confused. And Patch is probably thinking that I forgot about him. A dog lives the same way a child does. A child cries while a dog whines sorrowfully. And he barks either from anger or else joy. And he plays the same way. He looks you in the eyes and thanks you and licks you—and he growls; as if he were warning you, saying "stop now."

But then I remembered the lesson and that I had to pay attention because I already stood by the desk once.

When I was a grownup, I thought it was an easy thing to be an attentive pupil, to pay attention during the lesson and get good grades. Now I see how difficult it is. When I was a teacher, and I had a reason to be worried, I didn't pay attention during the lesson either, and no one was putting me in any corner. It was just the opposite—I became stricter and it had to be quieter in class so that I could ponder over my problem more easily.

Oh, Patch, Patch! You're small and weak and so they treat you indifferently, and even mistreat you. You aren't a life-saver who rescues drowning people, or a St. Bernard who digs out people from an avalanche. You aren't even a huskie. Nor even a smart little poodle, like Uncle's.

I'll go to Uncle with my dog. Let them get acquainted. A dog likes companionship too. I'm thinking: "I'll go to Uncle." I'm not thinking, but rather dreaming. Because I'm sure they won't let me keep him at home.

A grownup will say to a child: "You can't; I won't allow it," and will forget right away. He doesn't even know what pain he inflicts.

When I wanted to be little again, I only thought about games and that children are always happy, that they don't think about anything and aren't concerned about anything. But in reality, I'm suffering more over a stray, little dog than a grownup does with a whole family. But at last, the bell rang.

And we're giving the janitor the ten cents for the milk. But he says:

"I should wait for your ten cents! Only look at what that dog did." He's showing us what happened while Patch, locked up in a dark closet, is barking.

"That's nothing," I say. "Can I use this rag to clean it up?" I cleaned it up and didn't even feel any disgust.

And Patch recognized me because he became very excited. He almost ran out into the corridor. He's dancing around in a circle and jumping. He completely forgot about his plight. He could have been lying at this very moment, stretched out in the cold snow, dead.

"Well, go on, get out now," said the janitor, but corrected himself right away:

"Go now, boys, I don't have time."

A grownup will never say "get out" to another grownup; but it is often said to a child. Always, when a grownup gets busy over something, a child is in his way; a grownup jokes whereas a child is always the fool; where a grownup cries, a child weeps and sobs; a grownup is nimble but a child is clumsy; a grownup is pensive while a child is hurt; a grownup is absent-minded while a child's a chatterer and a fool. A grownup gets lost in thought, but a child gapes; a grownup does something quickly, but a child dawdles. It seems like a harmless language, but it's crude nonetheless. A whiner, a nuisance, a scamp, a brat—even when they're not angry, when they want to be good. It's too bad, but we've gotten used to such names. But, sometimes, it hurts us, such a disregard, and makes us angry.

Poor Patch—but maybe Snow would be a better name—again he's going to have to sit locked up in the dark for two hours.

"Maybe it would be better to keep him under my shirt; maybe he'll be quieter?"

"Silly," said the janitor and locked the door with his key.

I meet Mundek and he asks: "What kind of a secret are you hiding?"

He's jealous because he doesn't know. And so, I told him.

"So that's it?! And you told him first?"

"Well, I had to. He didn't want to loan me any money for the milk."

"I know, I know."

I feel sorry for Mundek because I would have been hurt too, if he told someone else his secret before me. But during the long recess, I ask him: "Do you want to see him?" But here, on the second floor, some boys were smoking and now they were trying to find out who it was, who was on the second floor.

And our janitor says: "I'm always chasing them away, but they always sneak back." And he's looking straight at us. I hid behind Tomczak. They would have noticed right away that I turned red. I suddenly felt warm. When grownups are asking a child about something, and he stammers or blushes, they think right away that he's either lying or he's guilty. While we blush at the slightest glance, from shame or fear, or else our hearts begin to beat fast all of a sudden. And some grownups even have the habit of telling us to look in their eyes. But there are some children who, even though they're guilty, can look the person straight in his eyes and lie outright. Those kind don't suffer. Only it's the worst for the sensitive child. He's not to blame but he suffers. Because the grownups yell at everyone. Right away they say: "all of you."

They threaten and yell at everyone.

"I know you now. Your alibis! Now I have you."

And the sensitive child takes fright and lives in constant fear. Like a rabbit. Even when he sleeps, the rabbit's afraid. And we too, have disturbing dreams. And we awake in fright. Something creaks in the middle of the night, and we imagine that a ghost is walking or, a murderer. Or, else, something appears in the window, or something is seen moving. You cover your head with the blanket; you're afraid to breathe, you're perspiring and thinking all the while: "What will happen if some cold hand touches me?" You recall the most frightening stories then, some terrible news from the newspapers. And it isn't only in fairy tales that horrible things occur. Because, of course, there are people without legs, without a nose; a man could lose his eyesight, go mad— someone's walking along the street when, suddenly, he falls down and begins having a fit, and there's froth coming out of his mouth; he was walking along as everyone else when it suddenly happened. A crowd of people gathers around and tries to help. but you they push away. And you don't want to leave; you have to look; you're so rooted to the spot, like a stone.

And then there's the black plague, galloping tuberculosis, eye infection and gangrene, blood poisoning? You don't pay attention to these horrors. Grownups say a lot of things on purpose so that children shouldn't listen and act up too much. And you can see that the car didn't run over you, or that you didn't fall out of the window, or that they didn't break your legs, or knock your eyes out. And then you stop believing them. Besides, you can't always be careful.

But just let such a night come and you remember everything immediately. Everyone's asleep; it's dark, or else, the moon's shining. And you're afraid again that maybe you'll start walking in your sleep along the walls and over the roofs.

It's strange. One time you're so brave that in the biggest fight or else, at night in a cemetery, you don't even blink your eyes, while at another time, the slightest nonsense frightens you. And it's hard to say whether you're brave or a coward.

And, in general, it's very difficult to know just what kind of a person you really are. Because when I ask myself whether I'm good like I ought to be, I really don't know. Then I'll remember some secret, but immediately I'll think:

"But others are worse even."

Even if someone seems to me more decent that I am, or better, still I don't know everything about him, what he does and thinks. Sometimes someone can pretend or doesn't do anything bad because he's afraid that he might give himself away.

Then there are those mysteries where you haven't even done anything bad. I guess children have these secrets the most. And they have to keep their secrets; they're not supposed to tell. Take me, for example, now. What's wrong in it that I took pity on a hungry and frozen dog? A frozen, little dog—a living creature.

Why is it that grownups forbid us so much?

Well?

We'll ask the teacher during a lesson: "Please Sir, permit us to bring Little Patch with us to class. You'll see, we'll be quiet and we'll pay attention."

But no. Nothing would come of that. Wisniewski would be the first to act up—and out of spite.

It's a pity that we're all together—the delicate and the crude ones, the diligent and the uninterested. Because of them, you can't keep any promises or keep your word. Because of them everything ends badly.

Because of them, grownups don't trust us, don't believe us, and treat all of us alike, indifferently.

Without them, it's true, there might be less laughter and joy, but life would be more peaceful.

And grownups think that we only like the trouble-makers, that we only listen to the worst ones, that whatever they tell us we do. That they spoil everyone!

It's not true. When we don't listen to a trouble-maker ten times, no one knows of this. But if we should do one thing with him—right away everyone's getting blamed. The world would really be in some shape if we always did what they wanted. And how would it really be if we didn't quiet them down, temper them.

How many times do you say: "cut it out—leave it alone—stop—don't do that. Or, "Hey, you'll be sorry afterwards."

And he'll listen to you, that trouble-maker. And, indeed, if grownups can stand him at all, then it's a feather in our cap.

Well, this is how it ended: it wasn't discovered who was smoking cigarettes on the second floor, and we didn't get to see our little dog.

Only, after school, the janitor tells us:

"Take him now and don't bring me any more dogs, because I don't have the time. You'll go marching to the office together with your dog the next time."

And we left: Mundek, I, and Backiewicz. And Patch—yes, let his name be Patch finally.

How happy he was when we let him go free. Like every other living thing, it is drawn to freedom—whether it's a man, or a pigeon, or a dog.

We deliberate, the three of us, what to do next. And Backiewicz agreed to take him until tomorrow while I, in the meantime, will ask at home. It was as if I resented Backiewicz though, when he was taking him home. He's mine, of course. It was I who warmed him up under my coat. He licked me first. I found him and brought him to school, and thought about him the whole time. While Backiewicz only gave ten cents; that's all.

God! is it just that some parents allow things while others don't? Everyone loves his family the most. But one knows that another father will allow something—and he resents it. He compares himself with others and it hurts him.

Why does Backiewicz take Patch and think nothing of it, while I have to plead first? And it will probably come to nothing.

That one is richer, while another is poorer and the richer one can buy and do whatever he wants—that's crazy. Freedom is more important than wealth.

98

And if you know that your parents really don't have any money, then you love them even more. Who's going to be angry because his father doesn't have work, or because he earns little? But when he spends money on unnecessary things and doesn't spare any for the child, thinks only about himself, and regrets spending a penny on his children—well, that's too bad; here, even a priest can't help. So why does Mundek's father spend money on drink and create scenes at home yet?

I feel sorry for Mundek and for my white Patch, that I worried about him so much, and now someone else is taking him home.

"You don't have to pay me back those ten cents," Backiewicz says.

"No thanks," I answer, "maybe even tomorrow I'll return them."

"If you're going to be mad then you don't have to give him to me."

"Come on, Doggie, let's say g'bye."

And Patch is trying to break loose, and he doesn't even understand that this is a parting. Only afterwards, he leaned against my chest with his paws and wagged his tail as if he were happy. Then he looked straight in my eyes. O-o-o-oh!

Tears filled my eyes.

And then he licked me right on my lips—as if he were   sorry too.

And I hugged him for the last time.

Until Mundek tugged me lightly by my pocket.

"Let's go already."

And we went quickly and I didn't even turn around.

Mundek talked about pigeons the whole time and about rabbits and magpies and hedgehogs. I only said a word or two. The trip home passed unnoticed. It happens this way: the time always seems to be the same on a clock, while with a person it's as if there were a completely different clock inside him, showing a completely different time. Sometimes an hour passes and you don't even notice it; sometimes it goes so slowly that it seems like it will never end. Sometimes you've just barely stepped inside school when the bell's ringing already and you're returning home. But when it went badly for you in school then you wait for the whole mess to end and you leave like a prisoner, and you don't even have the strength to be happy.

And so I say goodbye to Mundek, but something tempted me to ask:

"And did your ol' man get drunk again yesterday?"

Mundek turned red and answered:

"Do you think that my father gets drunk everyday?" Then he walked away so fast that I didn't have time to say anything else. But why did I say that? Sometimes you say something because you lose control of yourself and then you can't help it.

Once Papa told me a proverb: "The virtue of all virtues is to keep your tongue behind your teeth."

A very wise proverb. At the time I was angry over something, and I didn't like it. Because I said something which was the truth, and they scolded me as if I told the greatest lie. No one asked and I didn't have to say it. But it would have been insincere if I hid the truth inside me.

There is so much in life that is false. When I was a grownup, I got used to it; it didn't bother me anymore. If that's how it is, then that's that. It's too bad. But you have to live.

Now, however, I feel differently—it pains me again, that a person can't tell another person what he really thinks. Only you have to pretend constantly.

A lie itself can be either good or bad. But man is false—and that's probably the worst. He thinks one thing but says something else; it's one way when you're face to face with him but another behind his back. I prefer someone who is insolent, a liar, anyone but a false person—he's the hardest to recognize. I'll tell someone:

"You're lying." or "Don't show off." And that's it.

It's simpler, more honest somehow.

But a false person is so sweet and kind that it's difficult to catch him red-handed.

Well, I hurt Mundek. He took offense. I called his father "old man" and said that he got drunk. I said it crudely, just like a grownup would, in a way which would make a child feel ashamed, which would offend, and which you yourself don't even feel.

And here, I enter my gate and on the step is sitting the same cat which was there yesterday. I felt sorry for him and I wanted to pet him, but he jumped up on his legs. That means that he remembered. Maybe God is punishing me for the cat, by not letting me be able to keep Patch at home.

"How was it in school today?" Mama asks. She asks gently. Maybe she senses that she yelled at me yesterday for no reason at all.

"Nothing much," I answer.

"And did you stand in the corner?"
And then I remembered that I did.
"I stood by my bench," I say.
"And you say that nothing happened?"
"I forgot."
I take the knife and begin to peel the potatoes with Mama.
"What for?"
"I wasn't paying attention."
"Why weren't you?"
"I was day-dreaming."
"About what?"
I'm peeling quickly, as if I'm busy, and I don't answer.

"You see, it's not good to forget. A respectable child is ashamed to stand in the corner, and tries not to do it again. You know, the teacher puts you there to teach you a lesson, as an example: so that you would understand everything better. And when you forget, then the whole lesson of the punishment is lost. You have to remember your punishments."

I glanced at Mama and am thinking:

"Poor, dear Mama; she doesn't know and understand anything."

"She's poor and old," I thought in addition.

Because while Mama was sitting bent over, I saw that she has grey hairs and wrinkles. Maybe she isn't old yet, but she has a hard life. And I think:

"It's good to have a mother again. Children have their problems with parents, but it's much worse without them—it's bad—it's very sad and bad.

"But maybe you did something else in school?"
"No, nothing."
"You aren't lying, are you?"
"Why should I lie? If I didn't want to, I wouldn't have told you about the corner."

"That's true," Mama says.

And then it's quiet. But in such a way as if we were still talking. Because in my thoughts, I have a wish about my Patch, and Mama knows that I'm not telling her something, that I'm hiding something.

We, children, like to chat with grownups. They know better. But if only they didn't have so much against us. If only they were gentle with us. And not always complaining, grumbling, reprimanding, scolding and yelling. If Mama would have asked me the same thing another time: "Maybe you're lying?," I might lose my patience and maybe I would answer the same way, with the same words, but there would be anger in those words.

Grownups don't want to understand that a child answers gentleness with gentleness, and that anger immediately awakens in him something like revenge or spite. As if he were to say: "This is what I'm like and I won't be any different." After all, everyone, even the worst among us, wants to be better. And maybe bad children differ from bad grownups mostly in that they have already made an effort, have tried—they've tried but nothing's come of it and so, that's too bad. But we struggle and try and strive and make an effort and when it doesn't turn out well then they jump on us right away. And that annoys us very much. The more a person tries, it seems that it's good but, instead, it's "start over again from scratch." You get so angry at this and discouraged. It hurts very much. And, instead of helping us, encouraging us—you hit us and crush us right away. That's why we have such unlucky days, bad weeks. If it isn't one thing, then it's another and another—we just don't have any luck.

And the worst thing is when something doesn't turn out and you suspect us of ill-will. It happens that one doesn't hear well, or misinterprets, or forgets, doesn't understand or misunderstands. And you think that it's done on purpose. Sometimes we really want something good to happen, to make someone a surprise, something pleasant, but because we have no experience, it turns out badly—a harm instead, or a loss. We feel it ourselves, of course, and so why create a scene right away?

It's awful for a person who feels deeply.

And so, I'm moping around the house. I dusted the flower pots on the window sills. Then I started to dust the whole room. And Mama is surprised. And that's how we made up for yesterday's affair. Because who knows? Maybe I was a little at fault there too. You shouldn't be late for supper. But then, even saints committed sins.

"Go and play a little," Mama says, "why should you sit here?"

"I'll go and bring Irene home from the nursery."

"All right, go ahead."

I got dressed and am on my way, but I don't know myself why I'm going. Probably because of Patch. Well, and you have to take care of little children too.

I'm not a good brother. I take pity on a dog while I don't really love my own sister. Not only do I not love, but I don't even understand. Such a little child can only be a nuisance; she can only pester out of boredom. If I do play with her, it's as if I were doing her a favor. Otherwise, I yell at her and tease her. Exactly as grownups treat us, older children. It must be that we learn these things from them.

The three biggest reasons why we don't like little children are: first, that grownups tell us to make way for them whether they're right or not. Second, grownups tell us to set them a good example. And third, they tell us to play with them even though they bother us. In other words, because of a younger one, we often get scolded. And so, we suffer doubly: because of ourselves, and because of a younger child.

For example: I have something and she insists that I give it to her. If I want to, I'll give it to her of my own accord, because I know what you can and what you can't give her. But do grownups give in to us when we persist? They'll even yell at you; and if they should give in just to have peace at last, that's even worse, because they'll teach you that you won't get anything by being good. And such a little pet darling sees that you take his side and he learns to cry when he wants something. That makes you real mad.

Let him cry. Oh no! He screams as loudly as he can—of course, for everyone to hear, to create a commotion.

When a certain family lived here once, and the father didn't want to give his little girl something, she made a regular scene in the yard.

"All right now, be quiet," he says, "you make me ashamed and yourself too."

While she: "That's what I want to do! Let everyone know. Let the whole house gather around. Let the police come; let the ambulance come, let them write about it in the newspaper."

She probably got used to this when she was very little. Because that's how they behave. They holler and scream and grownups don't want to find out what is really the matter; they only want it to be quiet.

And always: "She's little; you should make way for her."

Yes. Make way for grownups and little children too.

A grownup will give you a spanking, and not always justly, but when your brother hits you, they immediately get concerned and fuss over you.

I made myself a wind-mill. I slaved over it half a day.

"Give it to me." She started to tear it out of my hands.

"Go away, or you'll get it."

"Give me, give me."

And what does Mama say? "You'll make yourself another one."

Maybe I will and maybe I won't. But let her ask; let her wait and let her not grab it and—Ma-a-a-a-o-o-o!

A person can hardly restrain himself, he's so angry. And she even wants you to hit her because then, for certain, she'll go and tell on you. And then you have a regular scene: "A fine brother! So big, too!"

When it's convenient—I'm small; when it's convenient—I'm big.

Or else, I'm not only to blame for what I do, but for what she does as well.

"You taught her. You showed her. She heard it from you. It's your example."

Did I tell her to imitate me like a monkey? If I set a bad example, let her not trail around after me, let her not talk to me, let her not play with me.

Al-e-e-e! Rather, I have to play with her. And how!

"Put your coat on otherwise she won't want hers either. You won't get a piece of sausage because she'll want some too. Take a nap because she won't go by herself."

They'll make you so sick of the child that you won't want to have anything to do with her. But no: you have to go and play. Well, all right.

There are games however where a little one can be useful. He can do something too. Only let him listen, let him not destroy the toys, let him understand that he can't do everything we can.

And you tell him: "Sit here, you'll be this and that."

And he doesn't want to. He wants to run around. But I'm the one who has to answer if he should fall down and get a bump or tear his clothes. And then he wanders around and only gets in the way.

For grownups, it's all the same whether a child is five years old or ten. If it's convenient—there's no difference: "Children, go and play."

And when it's convenient, then you're the older one, you have to play the nurse, and give in, and set an example.

Grownups themselves sow the seeds of discord among their children, and that's why there can't be any harmony. And that's why we older ones try to avoid the younger ones. And we only get close to them when we're already very bored or when we want to rid ourselves of even a smaller one.

But we're not without blame either. There's a lot of cheating among us. Just let a little one try to have something. Right away there'll be someone who will want to be his friend, who will try to wheedle it away from him. It looks like he's playing with the smaller one, until he gets what he wants—and then, he won't even look at him. And the little one feels proud that they're asking him for it, or else is ashamed to suggest that they return it. There are all sorts, among older ones and younger ones. That's why the better ones among the older children won't have anything to do with a smaller one, so that he wouldn't be suspected of anything; only the worst kind seem to go to the little ones.

And the older ones really set a bad example for the younger ones and spoil them. That's how the little person grows up into a trouble-maker. And afterwards, when he gets some sense, it's hard for him to break his habits, to change for the better.

I'm walking in the street and thinking. I look—and it's my Patch. I had to stop. But it was only my imagination. He wasn't even close in resemblance. And so, I'm thinking about Patch again.

"Maybe I shouldn't take him? Maybe it would be better for him there? Maybe Mama will let me keep him, but afterwards she'll be angry. Because, if they really wanted a dog, we would have one even without me. I'll wait a few days and see what Backiewicz will say, how Patch is behaving there. He made a mess in the closet at school. But he was locked up too."

And I don't know whether I should be concerned with my own happiness with Patch, or whether I should try to arrange a better future for him. But then, I've already done something. I saved his life and found him a home. Maybe now I should spend a little more time with little Irene?

I arrive at the nursery, and there are a lot of little children playing about. They're holding hands in a circle and are singing.

And the woman in charge says to me: "If you're going to stand there, why not join us." And she extended her hand and I joined in.

Another time I probably would have been ashamed and would have refused, but no one will see me now. I began to play. I began to joke from the very beginning, to create more laughter. I squatted down and made believe that I was little. Then I limped as if I had an injured leg. And I even tried to tease the woman, to see whether she'd get angry. Because, in any case, I could always leave. But the woman laughed too, and so I really played with them.

The little children were pleased and each one wanted to hold my hand. Well, not every one, because some where bashful— they didn't know me. But the proudest one among them was little Irene—that she has a big brother. And she began to take charge:

"You, this way, and you stand here..."

She thinks that I'll defend her if anything should happen. But I told her to stop it or else I would leave.

Little children have such a habit—if one of them knows that an older brother will come to his rescue, he'll be the first to start something and then run away. And he'll expect his older brother to take charge of him, protect him, fight for him. And his brother, if he's a bully, will gladly stand up for him and fight—he doesn't risk anything; in fact, he even feels magnanimous:

"Why did you hit him, he's little? I had to defend my brother."

He'll thrash his little brother himself four times as hard at another time—but now, he's the dear brother, the protector, the defender.

Then again, a decent person won't want to fight at all, but he's forced to, even though he knows that the little one isn't right. He's afraid too, because he knows he'll have to answer to his parents for his younger brother.

The woman in charge of the nursery has to go and write some kind of letter, and, therefore, she leaves me with the children. And they listened to me while she was in the other room.

Only one child was a nuisance the whole time. Afterwards, when I was telling them all the fairy tale about puss in the boots, the little boy kept disturbing me. I was so angry, I didn't know what to do. Mostly, because he was doing it on purpose.

And now, Irene and I are returning home. Suddenly I heard something rattle in my side pocket. And I find two cents. If there had been more, I would have left it for Backiewicz—but this isn't worth it. I gave them to Irene. She too, when she has something, shares it with me. Sometimes, I'll take it, sometimes I won't. Because if you take something from a little child, right away you're called a toady. That's how it is—a decent person always has to answer for something bad, when he isn't at all to blame.

If we could change something (though I don't really know what), then our childhood would be sweet indeed. We children need little to make us happy and we don't seem to have even that little bit. They seem to be concerned about us, those grownups, but it isn't really too pleasant for us in the world.

I'm walking along, and I feel good holding little Irene by the hand. I pay attention to how we should go: I choose the better route. And I feel older and stronger. And her hand is so small and soft, like satin. And her fingers are so tiny. You're even surprised yourself that at one time you love this little person while at another, you hate her.

She ate one piece of candy and offended me the other. I didn't want to, but I ate it and she looks at me and laughs, happy that she treated me.

It's nice sometimes to give something of your own, and not to always take, and take from older people. It's unpleasant too, when you want to give something to a grownup and he doesn't take it, or, he gives you something in return, something more expensive. It looks like he's paying for it right away. A person feels degraded then, like a beggar.

If only the world could be organized so, that everything would be done as a common exchange of favors. When I felt sad, Irene gave me the glass lens; and I bought her candy and she gave me some. A whole chain of favors.

Finally we returned home.

Auntie is visiting Mama and she says:

"O-o-o, your little calves are coming."

Why "calves," and not people? Did we do anything wrong that Auntie should call us little calves? Only cows have calves. Why did she use such a vulgar expression?

I'm annoyed at this and so I don't say hello at all. Mama even got angry:

"Why are you coming in like some thief? Why don't you say hello to your aunt:?"

"Why should I?" I say. "I was at her house only yesterday."

"That was yesterday, and this is today."

"And little calves don't say hello," I grumbled.

"What kind of little calves?" Mama asks, because she didn't hear, because you only hear and remember grownups' impressions.

Then Auntie burst out laughing.

"Oh, look at the proud one, will you! He's offended!" And she's getting up to kiss me, but I turned away. She's doing me a favor that she'll wet my face.

"Just ignore him, the good-for-nothing," Mama says.

Good. Let me be. I was offended.

And can't I be? If I won't defend myself now, then, when I grow up, I'll let myself be abused.

I sat down and pretended to be doing my lessons. I'm all but shaking from indignation. Then I remind myself that they laughed at me in the streetcar as well, and that I defended myself. Grownups think that a child isn't able to be offended. As if it were a game. Everyone knows what's pleasant and what isn't.

They say that children are stubborn. "He's stubborn and won't say hello."

That's right too.

"Say it this instant; do it right away."

No. It isn't out of spite at all and you would prefer to be punished rather than not to respect your own honor... And they shouldn't force you, because they'll only make you obstinate.

I'm sitting with my back turned and I'm writing. But not as fast as before. Am I becoming a child then in every way? And then it will be difficult for me in school again. Then I'll really have to pay attention during the lessons. That would be terrible.

And just then I hear a siren.

"Can I go?"

I look at Mama pleadingly and wait as if for a verdict. I don't know what I would have done, had Mama not let me. How often do grownups say without thinking: "No," and then forget; and how much misery do they impose—they don't know at all.

Why "No?" Well, why? Because something can happen, because they prefer to be left alone, because it's unnecessary; why then? It's such a small thing; so unimportant. They could say "yes" but they don't want to at all. And so, "no," and that's that.

And we know that it could be "yes," that this refusal is only accidental, that they would agree to it if only they would make a little effort to think about it, to look into our eyes, to see how much we want it.

And so, I ask: "Can I go?"

And I'm waiting. Grownups never wait this way for anything. Except maybe in jail—whether they'll let him out or not.

I wait and I imagine that if Mama didn't give me permission, I would never forgive her this. Grownups think that we ask for everything and that we forget right away. It's true that it happens this way sometimes, but it happens oppositely too, at other times. Or else, we never ask at all because, in any case, nothing will come of it, and we don't want to hear a coarse word. (Oh, and how it hurts, with what a sting, when they answer yet with some crude word.) Instead, we prefer to hide our hurt and we don't ask at all, or, we wait long and patiently when they'll be in a good mood, when they're completely pleased with us so that it would be awkward for them to refuse. And sometimes, this doesn't happen; and then we're angry both at them and at ourselves.

"Why did I hurry; maybe they would have let me another time?"

It seems that grownups have different eyes and view things differently. Because, when my friend asks me for something, I take one glance at him, and I know what to do. I decide right away, on the spot, or else I give him a condition, or question him exactly, or put it off until later. Even if I can't help him, I don't dare to refuse him curtly and without reason.

For instance: yesterday one boy said that he needed to go to the bathroom. But the teacher says: "Enough of that fidgeting. You could have gone during the recess." Well, I know they're fidgeting without reason—that's true. But is it his fault? I only take one look and I know. In the end, the teacher gave him permission, but towards the end of the lesson, she was yelling at him that he was fidgeting. She doesn't even remember that he went to the bathroom. But I know that he began to act up out of spite, because he suffered so much, was so afraid over what would have happened if he couldn't have waited.

Grownups don't know why we do things out of spite. They think that we behave this way because of being punished. We punish them too—with disobedience—if they deserve it.

Why then, do we behave one way towards someone and another way toward somebody else? If a different aunt called me a little calf, I wouldn't get annoyed—it could be a joke. but it wasn't the first time with this one. She has such a high-pitched voice and she likes to order one about. And she's so haughty. Let her be that way, but she likes to poke fun too and annoy us children.

She's probably annoyed herself that she has so many children of her own; but who's to blame? She shouldn't have them. "I have to scold them constantly. It costs so much. I give from my own mouth. I sacrifice myself."

She gives from her own mouth and she's as big as a barrel. A child means expenses; it can't be helped.

There are grownups who don't even notice us it seems.

"Good-morning, you little devil," he'll say, or, "Ho, ho, what a big man."

Just to say something. And it's obvious that he doesn't know anything more, and he seems to be uneasy. Or, if he should stroke your head, then it's done very carefully, as if he were afraid to break something or pull something off. These kind are strong and good and delicate people. We like to listen to them talk to other grownups. They relate some kinds of adventures, or something about war. We like them.

While others behave as if they don't have anything to do—either they make some practical joke or else, it's some sort of derision, some nick-name. Or else, someone will play some wild game with you. He's got a coarse chin and smells of tobacco and then he hugs you. Or, he squeezes your hand and laughs when it hurts. Or he may throw you up in the air and think that it's great fun for us.

"I'll throw you out the window...I'll cut your nose off...I'll snip your ears; then you won't have to wash..."

It's all silly and senseless. And you only wait for him to leave you alone. While women—immediately they're petting you and hugging and kissing you, either on the lips or else, they're hugging you so hard that your ribs hurt. And you have to be polite because she loves you. And when some older boy, who is around sixteen starts to play at being an adult, then it's really hard to bear. Either it all ends in tears or else, in a misfortune of some kind—from such tumbling.

It's best to be with your own kind.

Mama gave me permission to go to the fire. It's high time, too, because should the fire-engine already go by, you won't be able to find the fire.

"Only come home right away."

She probably had something to talk about with Auntie. That's why she agreed to it so quickly.

"And don't go tearing your shoes," Auntie added.

She always has to stick her nose into everything.

Who can guess what it means: "Come home right away."

I hurry because I'm afraid that I won't make it or that Mama might add something else, or Irene might want to tag along. You're never certain what can be waiting for you. And so, I grab my cap and I'm off. Four steps at a time. You can go down the stairs this way, but you have to use the railing, and sometimes you get a splinter. That's painful, but you risk it.

One boy knew where the fire was. Not far. A kerosene shop. They say that there's gasoline in the cellar. If it catches fire the whole house will blow up. The police are chasing the people back while the fire-engines and the helmets of the firemen are glistening from the light of the flames.

I don't want those drums of gasoline to catch fire—it would be a pity; the people would be left without a roof. And yet, when those people from the shop, the owners, aren't nearby where you can see them, you feel less sorry somehow. Because it would be great to see such an explosion with the whole house going up.

Why is it pleasant to watch terrible things? Some accident, a drowning, or a bicycle falling under a car, or when there's a fight, or they're catching a thief. Maybe that's why there are wars—people are fond of blood and danger.

A fire must be the most exciting thing... It's like a heroic battle.

And grownups too, like to run and gape—not only children. It's as if they can be of use while they tell us: "Go away. You're not needed here."

I stand in a different spot each time and think all the while whether it's time to return home, or whether I can still stand a while longer. It's impossible not to be at the fire until the end, even though I'm afraid of getting scolded at home.

They're saying that an ambulance is supposed to be coming, that a woman got burned. You can't see any more flames, only smoke. I won't wait for the ambulance. I won't be able to squeeze up that close anyway.

But here, suddenly, a flame leaps high up in the air. And a fireman is attaching a new hose on a ladder.

"If they open up with the water, I'll go."

But maybe the house is going to collapse at this very moment.

I even want it to end now. And the police push us farther back. Again, I don't see very much and I feel like going home. And they're talking and saying in the crowd that the fire-engine pump broke and that another's coming.

And here again a woman is running and screaming. They hold her but she breaks loose. And I see Felek and Bronek and Gajewski. And I already want it to end. But no one's moving away. It's hard to leave on your own, when everybody else is standing around, waiting.

A fire isn't a game. But we often have to interrupt something pleasant in the most exciting place, not to be late somewhere, or because they tell you to.

Grownups are the same way, really. When they go visiting and they're having a good time, six times they'll say: "Well, it's time to go home."

"Just a little while longer," they'll say too, the same way. Either after another glass, or one more dance, or another game of cards—and then they have to leave, because it's as if they were feeling sorry for the children who are sleepy or because they have to get up early the next day.

Love

At last the day of the party arrived. Mama got dressed up in the gown which the moths ate. But you couldn't tell; Auntie made it over real well. It was a name-day celebration and there were guests. It was a party with dancing. It began in the evening and I don't know when it ended, because I fell asleep in Carl's house.

Mary was there from Wilno. And I danced with her. It was Uncle Peter who told us to dance. I didn't want to at all. But Uncle Peter said:

"You're such a gentleman? The Miss comes to you all the way from Wilno and you don't want to dance with her?"

I got embarrassed and ran out on the stairs. How can a person talk that way? As if she came just to see me. She could have been embarrassed too. But Uncle grabbed me and raised me up. I try to tear away from him and kick my legs in the air. He got out of breath even, but doesn't let me go. I was very angry because I got even more embarrassed. Then he put me down and said: "Dance."

"Don't be such a dunce," Papa says, "dance with her. She's a guest, from Wilno."

I'm standing and don't know what to do. I want to run away but I'm afraid that he'll grab me again and start shaking me. And so, slowly, little by little, I straighten out my shirt and look to see if something didn't get unbuttoned, or torn.

And Mary only glanced at me and said: "Don't be ashamed. I don't know how to dance very well either." And she's the first to make a motion. She took me by the hand. There was a blue ribbon in her hair and such a big bow. Her hair was tied on the side with that bow.

115

"Well, let's go and try it."

I gave Uncle an angry glance, but he's only laughing. And everyone stepped aside for us and made way. The two of us are standing there. And Papa—I know that if I don't obey—he'll get angry and maybe even tell me to leave the party. I have no choice.

I began to turn with her. My head was buzzing, because it was already late, and I had sipped a little wine. And so, I said: "That's enough." But they're all shouting "more." I feel hot and confused while they make a spectacle. She doesn't stop either and so, we continue, until I'm really dancing to the music, to the rhythm.

I don't know how long it lasted. Until Mary says: "Well, all right, that's enough. I see that you don't want to."

"Why shouldn't I want to? Only my head began to spin," I say.

"I can dance the whole night," she says.

Then the elders begin to dance, and we're standing near the door. Mary and I.

"Warsaw is very nice."

"Wilno too."

"Were you ever in Wilno?" Mary asks.

"No, but our teacher told us about it in school."

She addresses me familiarly, but I don't know how to address her. There is order among grownups: strangers say "Mr.," "Mrs.," and that's the end. But we, children, never know. To one you say "You;" to another "Miss," or "Master." One doesn't know oneself, finally. We suffer a lot of shame because of this, a lot of trouble and concern. You have to avoid it somehow, and say neither this nor that.

She—Mary—just came to Warsaw for a visit, and is returning to Wilno. She'll be here for around a week.

"Did she come for long?"

"Who?"

"Well, uh, that lady, Auntie—your mother?"

"Oh! About a week."

The train ride lasts a whole night from here to there. I never rode in a train at night yet.

"I'd like to live in Warsaw always," she says.

"And I'd prefer Wilno."

I only said it that way, that Wilno is a nice city too. And then she began to name the different streets there, and I named those in Warsaw. Then it was the statues and different monuments.

"Come sometime, and I'll show you everything."

"All right," I answered stupidly. As if it depended on me alone.

Carl came up to us and we began to talk about school; the kind of teachers there were there and books, and the kind there were here. It was very pleasant. But Uncle Peter already noticed that we're standing around and so walks over to us quickly, to start that business all over again. Then they asked Mary to sing. She isn't bashful at all. She raises her eyes upwards when she sings, as if she were looking to heaven. And she's smiling.

Then, we talked again. Stephen says that they have three sleds in his yard; one is so big that two people can ride in it.

"Come over and I'll give you a ride," he says to Mary.

And they have a good slide there too. They have everything in their yard. I don't like it when someone brags too much.

And that's how the party ended. That woman, Auntie, took Mary and left.

"Maybe you'll go to bed now?" Mama says to me.

I didn't object to it at all, and only ask: "Where?"

"At the Gorskis," she answers.

These are Carl's parents.

"You have to go to school tomorrow."

And I see that Mama won't refuse if I ask to stay a little longer. But what would I do? I feel like sleeping and I'm bored.

Little Irene went to bed right after supper. And I went to sleep with Carl.

"Why do they talk so funny in Wilno?" he asks.

"I don't know."

"I wanted to ask that girl, Mary, but I was afraid she'd be offended."

"Of course."

"She has hair like a Gypsy."

"That's not true. Gypsy's hair is stiff, but hers is soft."

"How do you know?"

"Well, you can see, can't you?"

"But Uncle Peter said it was Gypsy's hair."

"All Uncle Peter knows is what he eats," I say angrily. He yawned, was silent for a moment, and then started again:

"We don't have anyone like that around here."

I don't say anything.

"She's a very nice girl."

I still don't say anything.

"And she sings really nice, too."

I'm waiting for him to turn over on his side. Since I'm his guest, it isn't very polite to show that I don't want to talk to him. Therefore I ask:

"Did you do your homework?"

"Oh, homework," he answered, yawned again, and added finally:

"Well, it's time to sleep. But why did you agree to leave the party right away? Maybe there'll be some fun there now?"

"What kind of fun? They'll only drink some more."

"Did you drink anything? Because I did."

Tomorrow in school, he'll be saying what a hero he is, that he drank two glasses of wine and that his head was spinning.

He turned over on his side, covered himself, and still asked:

"You're not cold are you? I didn't take too much of the blanket?"

"No, I'm all right."

When a person feels sleepy, anything irritates him. I feel a little awkward that I don't like Carl and, yet, he asks me if I'm cold. And why did I say that they'll only drink more? It isn't nice to judge grownups. That's simply the way it is: they are different and they enjoy themselves differently. If it weren't for Uncle Peter, then I wouldn't even have spoken to Mary. How timid we are about everything. We're always concerned not to say or do something silly. There's always the feeling of uncertainty, whether it will be all right this way, or that they won't laugh.

I don't know myself anymore whether it's worse when they laugh at us or yell.

It's the same everywhere—at home and at school. You pose a question, ask about something, make a mistake or something—and right away they laugh and scoff at you. Everyone wants to be the smartest and only waits to ridicule and humiliate you.

This concern not to become the laughing-stock makes you so tongue-tied, so uncomfortable that you constantly feel uncertain; and the more careful you are, the easier it is for you to do something foolish. It's exactly like being on ice: the one who's afraid the most, falls down the most.

"Well, tomorrow we have to make a sled," I thought and then fell asleep.

And I barely fell asleep when, here, they're already waking me up. I slept for several hours, but it really seemed like much less.

I rub my eyes at breakfast and don't feel like eating.

"And maybe you won't go to school today?" Papa says teasingly. He thought that I'd be glad not to have to go. But then he adds:

"Fun's fun but school's school."

I inspect my school-bag carefully, not to forget anything—a pen or something. Because when you're sleepy, you have to be careful. But everything's there. And I leave.

I'm walking and thinking to myself that I'm riding to Wilno. I'm riding the whole night. Sparks are whizzing by outside the window—fiery zigzags, flashes.

I was thinking about this trip on the way to school and during the lessons. During the second hour, I felt like sleeping, and I completely forgot that I'm in class, and I begin to hum quietly—under my nose.

"Who's singing?" the teacher asks.

I didn't recover myself, even then, and only looked around to see who's singing. But Borowski tells on me.

"You were singing?" she asks.

"No."

Because I really didn't notice. And then I completely forget and begin to sing again. Probably even louder than before, because the teacher's very angry.

"Maybe now you'll say that it wasn't you?" says Borowski.

"I was," I say.

Only now do I realize that it was me really, this time as well as before.

The teacher looked at me in surprise: "I didn't know that you could be spiteful and that you could tell a lie."

But didn't she notice herself that I, too, have a surprised look on my face, that I'm confused myself? Why, I like the teacher, and she's good to me. Why would I do a thing like that? I lowered my head and turned red. Why bother to explain, she won't believe me anyway. Now I realize that a person can shout something suddenly or whistle like in a dream. And so I say immediately: "I did it out of spite. I'm a trouble-maker." That's an awful word, "trouble-maker." That's worse than "bully," worse than anything. It's offensive somehow. I don't like the word "discipline" either. In gym, for example. Subordination—discipline. I immediately feel as if they are going to punish, to beat you with a strap, or a belt.

"Spoiled brat."

"Brat" is also an ugly word. And the word "pup" too. You think of a dog-kennel right away.

There are indelicate words which shouldn't be used in school. You can often dislike a person because of some unpleasant word, one which is repeated a lot.

At first, the teacher told me to go to the corner but then she changed her mind and ordered me to the blackboard instead. She told me to solve a problem there. It was a very easy one. I knew the answer at once. I added it up quietly to myself and say:

"Fifteen."

The teacher pretends that she didn't hear. I'm annoyed, and I say:

"It'll be fifteen, won't it?"

"When you do it, you'll know. And do it for the whole class," she says.

I begin to go over it unwillingly. And then I got mixed up. The boys started to laugh.

"Go to your place. I'll mark a "D" down for you."

But Wisniewski interrupts and asks: "Should he go to his seat or to the corner?" I'm going and I couldn't help it since Wisniewski purposely stuck out his elbow—and so I gave him a shove. He yells with all his might: "What are you pushing for?" The lout. He was afraid that the teacher wouldn't notice. But the teacher hesitated whether to harass me further or to punish him. And then, the whole class began to act up. When they're sitting quietly, then it's quiet; but when it starts with someone, then immediately—comments, jokes, banter, laughter and commotion. Then it's hard to calm the class down. And the first one, the one who starts it, answers for everyone.

"Let them do what they want."

I put my head down on my arms and pretend that I'm crying. You do that often. That's the best. Then they leave you alone. By I'm not crying, although I'm suffering very much, because I'm very unhappy.

Suddenly I had the thought: "If Mary were a teacher, she'd be different."

Because if you misbehave very badly, you can be punished in a completely different way—and not be given a "D" in recitation. The boy who stammered at the blackboard after me, and who stumbled over the same problem, also arrived at "fifteen" in the end.

"No, Mary wouldn't have done it that way. But she's small, and she's leaving. She's going to ride the whole night. To Wilno. And I won't see her. Maybe never again. She'll never sing again. And she smiles so sweetly and has a blue bow. Her hair is soft too, not at all like a gypsy's."

The teacher must have been very angry, because during the recess she comes up to me:

"If you're going to have flies in your nose in class again, I'm going to report you to the principal. And I'm not going to defend you anymore."

And she walked away. She didn't give me a chance to defend myself. But if she had? What then? What would I have said?

That I like Mary?

Death rather than that!

"Flies in my nose!" I don't have any kind of flies in my nose. The teacher reproaches you over something that happened before. You shouldn't remind a person about the favors you did for him. Grownups should remember that that only irritates and angers the most. It means they think that we easily forget, that we don't know how to be grateful.

But it's they who forget. We remember very well. A year, even longer. Every rudeness and injustice, every remark, every one of their good deeds. We weigh everything honestly—and they have in us either an ally or an enemy. And we can forgive a lot too, if we notice any kindness and sincerity. I'll forgive the teacher too, when I calm down.

Mundek comes up to me and starts joking. He sees that I'm down-cast and he wants to cheer me up.

"Why should you worry about arithmetic? You'll get five As and that D'll run away from fright. You're so good in mathematics."

"A-aw, let up," I said quietly.

I go out into the yard, but I don't play. It all seems silly to me now, running around.

"How nice it would be if all the girls looked like her. And maybe we'll really take a trip to Wilno? Maybe Papa will get a job there? Anything can happen."

I took a book out of the library. Historical tales. I'll read them.

I return home alone. Mundek couldn't wait. And walking, I kick a piece of ice a little ways. You have to be careful kicking it, otherwise it could go off to the side somewhere. And I zig-zag behind it. Not to get held up, to be always ahead of it. It's the worst when it hits the curb—then it always goes off to the side, or else you have to turn back. I told myself that I could return for it ten times.

But I meet Papa and he was angry that I was ruining my shoes. I enter the gate and, here, children are playing with their sleds. I join them, but it isn't much fun. When you're worried about something you can still play, that's true, but every now and then you recall what's on your mind. It's as if someone were following you, saying: "Did you forget? Don't you remember?"

That's not your conscience; it's only a troublesome thought. Your conscience is something entirely different—it's something threatening—"You're afraid of God Himself."

One boy says that there is no God at all, that people only dreamed it up. He says that he knows for sure. He wanted to bet even—such a dunce.

I gave them two rides on the sled and they gave me one. And that's enough.

I sat down near the window and looked at the pictures in the book. I don't like them. The first picture is a heroic one. A knight on a horse. A battle. Missiles are falling and bursting everywhere, while he has his sword raised high and is looking like a doll—so stiff and straight.

Does it happen that way accidentally, that everything seems worse for a child? He's a good artist for grownups, but a poor one for children. And short stories are written as if they were doing favors; anyone writes them, poems and songs too. He whom the grownups don't want to listen to ends up with the children.

But it's we who really love stories the most, and pictures and songs.

They called me and told me that they were going to make a new sled, that I should give them my two boards, some rope and a piece of sheet metal.

When I gave them the metal they made a sour face, and complained that the rope was very short. But it was strong.

One board went for the seat, and the other to strengthen the underside. If there were more metal, you could line the whole bottom with it and then it would be easier to pull. It's good that there's a little in front at least. And I gave them nails too: I found one long, straight one in the street.

Everyone remembers what he gave, because then he has as much right to the sled according to what he gave. It's pleasant to make your own and have it for yourself. Then you don't owe anyone anything. But children rarely own anything really.

My clothes seem like mine, but my parents bought them. You're responsible for your books and pads both at home and at school. Everyone examines them and has the right to interfere. It's permissible for the teacher to roll up my notebook into a tube, but just let one of us try it. Right away they'll say that we don't take care of our things. Because everything has to be exemplary with children.

Partnerships are no good. We have to quarrel, of course. The one starts to give rides to someone, the other to someone else. One pushes or else, tumbles—you tell him that he's going to break it. But he's not concerned. He gave a few boards and so he has a right too.

Or else, he doesn't want to push at all; he only wants to sit like a prince. We argue often, that's true. But just think how easily we forgive everything...

How many law suits grownups have. While we only complain. But grownups don't like our complaints. They decide things in such a way as to be rid of us faster, or else, the one they like more is right, or the younger one, or else the older one's right, or the girl, or they're both guilty because it isn't nice to quarrel.

Maybe, sometime, people will live in peace and friendship; but not now, not yet.

He'll take offense over the slightest thing and then, immediately it's:

"If not, then give me back my boards and nails."

He knows that we won't give them back. What are we supposed to do, knock apart the whole sled? And what about all the work that went into it? Are you supposed to look for another partner and then go through the whole thing all over again?

"Children like to make things."

Of course they do, and when they make something they want it to last.

A child will draw something, and someone will go and tear it up as a silly joke—that's a shame. I found a stick and some string and made a whip—I don't want them to break it. If it's a sled then let it be. Sometimes it's good to break the thing you've made, because then you can make a better one. But you have to know from the start that you want to try again, and that's why you do it. Either because you have better materials or else, tools.

How can you make a sled without a hammer? We had to bang with a rock. If it were only a good one though. There is one but it's in the pavement. We even tried to dig it out and we planned to put it back later. Had the watchman seen us through, he would have given it to us but good. You wouldn't dare show your face around the yard for a week afterwards!

And so, I'm banging the nail with a round stone—it's uncomfortable and I hit my finger so hard that a little black spot appeared. And too, I tore my skin between the fingers with a piece of wire. Now, when I bend my finger it hurts. In one place it was necessary to pull the boards together with some wire, because we needed a long nail but used three small ones instead. And so, the board split. It had to be pulled together again.

And something's always breaking and you have to always be fixing it.

"O-o-o-h, they made a sled, and they won't let me have a ride."

"Then make a better one yourself."

"If I wanted to, I could."

"Then want to."

"When I feel like it."

"Beat it now and don't be so smart. If you don't like it, don't look then."

"You won't let me look?" he says.

"No, I won't."

One of us is working on the sled while the two of us are pushing him away. Until Franek says:

"Let him go. Help me instead because I can't do it by myself."

"Well, why is he standing around then, wising off?"

"Oh, let him. He doesn't have a sled, so he's jealous."

"Boy, I should be jealous of that thing, that scraper!"

Sometimes there's a fight from such a quarrel, and sometimes, such a quarrel is even useful. As it is now:

"You can't do anything without a hammer."

"Well, get one if you're so smart."

"I should give it to you so's you can break it."

"Do you have one?"

"Sure I do."

Then you bet him to see if he's really telling the truth. But he ran and got it.

"Is it your hammer?"

"Whose then?"

"Maybe you took your father's?"

"Well I did, not you!"

And if he should take it without permission and there's a scene—then everybody'll get it. And he has nails too.

"I'll let you use them if you let me ride it."

We shouldn't have agreed—he's such a spoil-sport. But time is precious and everyone wants at least a little ride. So we agreed. It's too bad though. Even the hammer won't help when the board's split. And he's heavy and he's riding it in such a way that it looks like he wants to break it on purpose.

All that work for nothing.

And again a quarrel. And so, I go home.

It's sad, sad, sad.

Little Irene is looking at me and she sees that I have a problem. And so, she doesn't ask me to play with her. She pulls the little stool up close to me, sits down on it and rests her little hand on my knee.

I don't stir. I'm only thinking:

"If Mary were my sister."

And I know that it's a sinful thought because it would seem that I'd want Irene to die so that I could have a different sister. I closed my eyes and put my hand on her head. And she immediately laid her head down on my knees and fell asleep. And I said a little prayer quietly, to myself: that Irene should live and be healthy and that Mary should be happy.

Well, that's how it is: I'm in love with Mary.

What a wealth of things goes on inside a person, what a variety! When you look around you, you see houses and people and horses and cars. A thousand or a million different objects; living and non-living. And a person has these same objects in his thoughts, in his mind. In man. I shut my eyes and I see them just as they are: houses, people, horses. Yes. And each object has a lot of different properties: a big house, a beautiful horse, a kind person. And the object with its qualities depends solely on whether people like it, whether I do or not.

That's how it is right now, at this moment—such a variety. I like Patch one way, my parents another, Mundek still another, and Mary from Wilno yet another.

But really, what can I say: I like, I like very much, I love. And that's it.

But I feel that its different.

And, as if on the very summit—there's God.

It's all very strange.

If I weren't a grownup already once before, maybe I wouldn't even have known. But now I know that children love too, only they don't know what it is called. And maybe even they're ashamed to admit it. No—it's not that they don't want to say it, but rather, they're ashamed to admit it to themselves, and only say that they "like."

They're even afraid to say it.

"That girl's nice. I like her. She's sweet."

Because grownups make fun of love very easily. And it is here precisely where you see how indelicate they are. They'll say:

"Ah, the prince and his lady."

Or: "Well, go ahead and kiss."

Or: "They're engaged."

Or even worse: "Husband and wife."

As if it weren't allowed to like someone. To talk to someone, to look or play together at some game or shake hands on parting. Only so that no one should ask about anything, or question. And that no one should notice anything.

What's the point, when you can't.

I ask as if unwillingly: "Is Mary a nice name?"

Or I'll say that she has a nice blue ribbon in her hair. Or: why does she have dimples when she laughs.

Let me just ask or say something like that, and they'll start snooping about:

"Do you like her by any chance? Maybe you'll marry her?"

Stupid jokes and silly laughter.

Because I know.

There are those kind who only mimic. They want to ingratiate themselves, to fawn, and so, they'll take the girl under the arm and: "My wife, my betrothed."

Grownups want us to be wise, as if they don't like our foolery while, at the same time, they force us to joke.

They don't know how unpleasant it is for a living being to make a fool of himself. One child is really broken by it, while another only bears a grudge towards you, an ill-will.

I'm sitting quietly, thinking. And just like me, thousands of children in various little rooms at dusk, are reflecting about the strange and sad things in life. About what is going on inside them and around them. And grownups don't know these musings of ours. Mostly it is:

"What are you doing there? Why aren't you playing? Why is it so quiet?"

A child runs around, makes noise, looks at a lot of different things and afterwards wants to converse with himself in quiet. And only one, one out of a thousand finds help in a grownup. Or in a friend.

Take for example, how strange dreams are. Little Irene is asleep and she isn't aware of anything. Or else, she'll have dreamed something, because she sighed. She, too, probably has children in the nursery whom she likes and maybe also doesn't want to tell about it.

I compare myself with Irene, and I recall how it was when I was a grownup and I see that we're all alike, the same. A mature person is child-like, while a child is like a grownup. Only we haven't come to an understanding with one another.

So...

I saw Mary again.

Mary visited us just one more time. She didn't even take her coat off. They say that they have to go, that they only came to say good-bye.

Once—the first time, to say hello and then, right away, good-bye.

I'm standing near my flower-box where I planted some peas. One sprouted. It already had four leaves. Two here and two there. It's really pleasant to sow seeds and see how they sprout.

You water them. And from the water and the seeds a plant starts to grow. And it's so tiny. From nothing, seemingly, something.

I'm standing holding a post-card: on it there's a picture of an angel with wings standing beside two children who are near a precipice. A bottomless abyss. The children are bent over the edge, gathering flowers, and the angel is watching over them so that they shouldn't fall.

That other aunt came with Mary. This is the first time in my life that I've seen her. She's a distant relative.

I'm thinking: "If Mary starts talking to me, I'll give her this post-card. If she doesn't, I won't."

I bought it for her because I knew she would come though I was afraid I might be in school then. I run home right after school—every day this way.

"What's your hurry?" Mundek is asking.

"Was school let out early?" Mama is surprised.

But I don't answer. What could I tell them?

Mary is wearing a white hat made of down, and she has on a similar collar. And her hair is in curls.

Her mother is talking with my mother—something about acquaintances in Wilno.

But Mary is silent. Because I kissed her mother's hand quickly, that aunt from Wilno, and went straight up to my flower-box. And she stood there, leaning against her mother.

I took the post-card out of a book. The one with the angel on it. And Mary immediately came over to me. She hurried so, as if she were pushed. And I hurriedly replaced the post-card in the book; I felt myself blushing because I got more confused.

She was standing and shielding her face with her muff which was also made of the same down; and I laughed. And she did too. Then I turned around, pretending that I was looking at the flower-box.

Irene came running up showing her a doll.

"Look, she has shoes," Irene says.

I turned back again and Mary took the doll and asks: "Does she close her eyes?"

"No," I answer, "little dolls don't close their eyes."

Then Mary came up quite close now and says that even little ones can close their eyes. It's only when they're absolutely small that they can't.

"I'm leaving already," she says.

I get alarmed that it's right now, at this moment, and I quickly take out the post-card with the angel on it. I'm afraid I won't have time, that I won't be able to give it to her.

"Is it nice?" I ask, showing it to her.

"It's nice," she says quietly.

And very quietly I say: "Maybe you'd like to have it?"

I didn't want Irene to see. Because little children like to butt in. And then maybe she'd say something aloud.

But Mama was talking with Auntie and they didn't notice or see anything.

"Write something, as a remembrance," Mary says.

She asks with such a pleading voice and is looking to see whether I agree. It turned out very well. I quickly wrote: "A souvenir from Warsaw." And I press it with a blotter.

"Oh, you'll smear it," she exclaims.

"Look, it didn't at all."

I said "look." It means that I addressed her familiarly. But the letter "s" did really get smeared a little.

"That's all right," she says and then, a little later, "write for whom and from whom, too."

"Why?"

Mary was thinking for a brief moment. She leans her head to the side a little and says: "That's the way it's done."

But I write: "For Mary from Wilno."

And I wrapped it up in a silver wrapper from a chocolate bar. I had everything prepared. But I saw that it shone through yet and so, I tore a page out of my pad and wrapped it up in that too.

"O-o-o-o, you're tearing out a page," she says.

"That's nothing."

"Take your coats off," Mama says.

"No, we really have to go right away," Mary's mother answers. And here, Mary took the post-card, all wrapped up, and stuffed it in her muff.

"Which letter do you like to write best of all?" she asks.

"Capital 'R'," I tell her.

"And I like capital 'W'." Let me have a piece of paper and I'll write it for you. But with a pencil. We'll see who writes nicer."

And she writes it. And I do too. But I really don't try very hard. Do I want hers to be nicer?

"Well, whose is nicer?" she asks.

She laughs and she has such straight teeth, and so white.

"You wrote better on the post-card," she says.

I blushed: "Sometimes it comes out, and sometimes it doesn't."

We write "Warsaw, Wilno"—different words and then numbers.

"I don't like to write eights," she says. "Somehow, the curve always comes out wrong."

"That's true. Eights rarely come out. Then too, it's difficult for her to write in her coat. And so she glances at her mother and says:

"Should I take my coat off?"

But they have to go already. Mary wants to tear that page up, but I don't let her.

"Why do you want that?"

"Let me have it."

"But why?"

"For a souvenir," I say quietly.

"O-o-o-h. What a funny souvenir. I'll send you a nice card from Wilno."

But she left the page. Then I showed her my flower-box. If she'd only want it. But how would she travel with a flower-box on the train? And Mary strokes every leaf with her finger.

"Well, we're going," her mother says. And she got up. Mary went up to her mother quickly. We didn't say anything more. I stayed near my flower-box.

And we talked for some time yet, standing this way. Well, maybe not too long. Though I already wanted them to go.

I'm a little nervous about the farewell. Really:

"Well, children, say good-bye to one another."

I turn away even more.

"What's this, you're not going to? And maybe you quarreled already? You won't kiss on parting?"

"I don't kiss boys," Mary says.

"Oh, you," says my mother. "Won't you sing something for us before you go?"

"I can sing."

"When we come another time. You'll only get your throat all warmed up now."

Mary gave Mama and little Irene a kiss, while she only stretched her hand out to me. And so gracefully. She didn't even smile. And in her gloves, too.

And they left.

"You're a boor," Mama says. "At least that Mary's a little lady. You don't know anything."

I'm grateful to Irene. I kissed her—I drew her close to me and kissed her head.

"You were real polite, Irene," I tell her.

And I begin doing my homework. I feel good and calm. It went off well with the post-card. It was a nice one too. At first I wanted to buy one with flowers on it then a landscape; a forest with a house near it and a horse standing beside the house. There were two other ones that were nice, but one had "Happy Birthday" printed on it. The one with the angel was probably nicest. There were mountains on it, and a precipice, and flowers, and this guardian angel.

It sounds terrible: Guardian angel. It ought to be different: "Protector"—do I know though?

When I'll have some money, I'll buy myself one just like it. Because Mary probably won't send one—she'll forget when she finally returns home.

I'm copying over a poem for tomorrow. Irene's doll is lying beside me. Everything began from that doll. And the flower-box with those four little leaves. When it grows up later, new leaves will come out a little higher, and these four will be on the bottom. And they'll probably be the first to fall off. Should I wait until they turn yellow and fall off themselves, or should I tear them off now while they're still green and dry them as a souvenir? For the time being, I'm not sure yet what to do.

I'm copying. I write very carefully. There was one capital "W" in a section. I made an attempt to write the best I could and I don't know whether a capital "R" is the nicest or the most fun to write, or the capital "W."

And I'm looking at the page on which we wrote those letters.

Well, it's too bad. I'm in love with her and we'll never see one another again. Just a page with tiny letters on it and four tiny leaves... But maybe she'll really write? And maybe I'll dream about her? Or maybe I'll see a girl on the street who will look like her. That's how it was with Patch.

Girls aren't nice. They're stuck-up, quarrelsome, and they make faces. They like to pretend that they're grownup and that boys—that's only mischief-making. They avoid us and, at the same time, want to be with us—as if they're doing us a favor. And when one of them by some chance willingly plays with us— then it happens that she's even worse than we are: she's a real tom-boy.

Well, yes. There are also those kind who are more delicate. There's a dress, and a bow, and beads, and different kinds of ornaments. It looks nice. But if a boy should try it—it would look silly. Because there are even boys with very long hair. Like dolls. Aren't they ashamed at all?

Yes. But should we make way for them? That you can't hit or push girls? "She's a girl," they say at once.

And that creates a resentment in us, discontent. And even hostility.

And why not?

When boys and girls study together in school, and a boy complains to the teacher about a girl, they say: "You're a boy, and you can't handle a girl yourself!"

If that's the case, then I take care of myself the next time. And again there's a big scene. And, in truth, you really don't know what's the right thing to do.

If only grownups didn't constantly remind us about the boy and girl "problem," we'd probably forget about it, or not think about it. Oh, no! Would they let you forget it, do you think? They talk about it as if there's no difference at all but, meanwhile, it comes out just the opposite.

It's unpleasant that I have to have such thoughts. It's too bad, but I can't lie. Mary, of course, isn't to blame. Or maybe it's this way only in Warsaw?

She wrote though. She really wrote. She kept her word. She sent me a post-card of the Black Madonna. And her address, and stamps, and everything. She wasn't ashamed to write to a boy.

She's bold. And she's not ashamed to sing either; and she was the first one to say that she would dance.

And she really wrote. And I put the post-card together with the page and the leaves. One leaf broke.

132

And there was an outing. Not by train, but on foot over the bridge to the park. It was wonderful. We wanted to walk four abreast down the middle of the street, and not in pairs, where there would only be pushing and shoving. But the teacher didn't let us. She was right. Because, right away, they'd break ranks and it would be a mess. Somebody kicks you from behind, another lingers, one goes off to the right somewhere, another to the left. They don't even walk in pairs, in order, in step.

It felt good. Two wagons and a car had to stop while we crossed at an intersection. It felt good that we, too, meant something, that they have to stop and wait.

I'm walking with Mundek. It's very important to choose a good partner to walk with, and to know who's in front and who's behind.

It was the best on the bridge because the water was frozen.

"There are those kind who swim through a hole in the ice."

"Wouldn't you be afraid?"

"Of what?"

"B-r-r-r, it's c-o-l-d."

"What of it, if it's cold?" I say.

It's fun at least to try to show that you're not afraid.

"You can make ice from water, or steam."

"Is that so strange?"

133

"And isn't it strange that a fly can walk on a wall and fish breathes in water?"

"Or a frog. It comes from a tadpole and that's that."

That's how we mused. As if someone could create all that? And if it wasn't God, then who?

Mundek and I are talking, imagining that we have a boat—we took some bread and cheese and apples—and we're going on a trip to Gdansk. We're going by way of the tributaries of the Vistula, past hills and dales, and historical sites.

We're talking in fun, but it sounds like a lesson, or an exam.

School is good. It allows a person to think for a long time about a lot of different things. You discover one thing in geography, another in biology, in history—and you have no idea even, how it all comes in handy in thinking.

"Shall we go to Gdansk or to Cracow?"

"E-e-h, it's hard to go against the current."

"Then in a motor boat."

Each school could have its own boat. It's standing in port somewhere while we're standing guard. Every day four others take their turn: day and night. And when the river stirs up, we let out the sails right away—and continue our journey.

One class goes for a week, and then another one goes. And we take turns: in the cabin, at the sails, or the steering wheel.

And we don't know ourselves whether it should be a schooner, a liner, a motor launch, or a scow, or even a raft.

The sun's reflecting sharply off the snow.

And it's very white in the park.

Only then do we begin to run around. Some even want to take their coats off, but the teacher doesn't allow it. But you get hot running around and then, we run around in our playground without our coats.

We don't cause much trouble though, because we don't want the teacher to yell. Anger is the worst thing when it ought to be gay and pleasant.

The teacher scolds one person, and everyone feels it. It rarely happens with grownups that when they're enjoying themselves some sort of disturbance occurs. It happens frequently with us. There seems to be one in every crowd.

And today, it's Kalicki. The teacher told him to walk with Rudzki. But he didn't want to from the start; they don't like one another. And Kalicki shoved and pushed him the whole way. The teacher got real angry that we're walking like a mob and said that she won't go with us again, that people were looking, and that it's shameful. And Kalicki, out of spite, gets under a wagon and the teacher's afraid that they'll run him over. But he goes to and from school every day by himself and no one watches him. Let him go alone. But I know, of course, that you can't, because if you let one go, then all the others will wander off.

And in the park they didn't come together right away; you had to prod them to return. But we came such a long distance and we wanted to stay longer. It was nice and you didn't feel like leaving. That's how it was. Some obey and are coming together. But you notice that one boy is still missing, and it's boring to stand alone, or else, you go and look for him. And those who have gathered see that others are still playing and their feet are freezing. And so, they get impatient.

"Let's go already."

They regret that they listened and formed so quickly. Those over there are still running around while these have to listen to the teacher getting angry.

They stand and stand and again they slip away. And the others look and see that only a few have formed and so they don't hurry. Everyone wants to be the last one, not to wait.

I wouldn't have gotten annoyed there. If the teacher began to move away with at least three pairs only, the others would have had to catch up and, little by little, they all would have gathered. Maybe one person would say:

"Let them go. I can manage my way home by myself."

But he'd be afraid to go alone for certain, because he'd get punished, and so even he would catch up. If not, then it's only one person. You shouldn't get angry at everyone right away.

If the grownups only asked us, we'd advise them correctly and not only on one thing. Why, we know better what bothers us; we have more time to think about and observe ourselves; we know ourselves better; we're together more often. One child may not know much but, in a crowd, someone can always be found who understands better.

We are experts of our own lives and affairs. We're silent though, because we don't know what can be said and what can't. We're afraid not only of grownups, but even more so of our own peers who don't want understanding, who don't want order, who prefer to fish for their own profit and advantage in those troubled waters of dissatisfaction and discord.

If I were a grownup I'd immediately say: "Anarchy and demagoguery."

Well, and what kind of solidarity is there? Everyone has someone whom he likes a lot and also some who are just nice pals; but he also has some who aren't so nice or who are indifferent; and he even has a pair of enemies.

Sometimes it happens that there's someone that everybody likes, or else someone who likes everybody. Otherwise, everyone's mostly afraid. The one who's strong can make his weight be felt and he can do whatever he pleases. Or else, there's someone whom the teacher likes very much.

And so, returning home from the outing, I told Mundek about Mary from Wilno.

"You know, Mundek, I got a post-card from Wilno. Flowers. Forget-me-nots. A very nice card."

And later:

"From a certain girl."

I told him what her name is and what grade she's in.

"Only remember, it's a secret."

I told him that I danced with her at the name-day party and that she sings beautifully. And that she has dark hair.

"You see, Mundek. And that time you were angry that I told Backiewicz first about Patch. I had to, you know, because he didn't   want to loan me any money. And I didn't know you well then either."

And we're talking this way, our arms around each other's shoulder, and Mundek says that he likes a certain girl too.

"Because she's always sad."

"My Mary though, must be happy."

On the bridge we weren't saying anything any more. Only later:

"You aren't angry that I talked about your father that day?"

I didn't think he'd hear because, just at this moment, a truck went by. An army truck—it was a heavy one. The chains were clanking so. Three soldiers were sitting in it while the driver was a civilian. I don't know why. And one of the soldiers had a dog. The dog rested his head on the railing and his head was bobbing up and down. He had such a scared look.

But Mundek heard: "I'm not angry," he says, "only don't say it anymore. It's not very nice. I sometimes think that my father can be heaven-knows-what. But everyone knows what he is. And it hurts when they say it."

"I didn't mean anything," I say, "It just came out."

And now, I'm really Mundek's friend. I'll bring the post-card too, and show it to him. I apologized for what I said and told him my own secret. I didn't want him to think that I only wanted to know everything about him. And probably, I'll ask him to come over to my house.

How funny it is when grownups tell us to apologize. You just did something—and immediately: "Go and apologize." Don't worry. If I know that I'm wrong, I'll apologize, but later sometime. I'll choose the time myself when that will be possible. Otherwise, it comes out false and sounding like a lie.

And Mary wrote in a funny way:

"Dear Cousin. I'm in Wilno and I'm not going to school. I rode the whole night and caught a cold. And I have a fever. I kiss you 1000,000,000,000 times. Your loving Mary."

I'm ashamed to show Mundek this post-card.

Well, and the teacher told us to write a composition about our trip to the park. It had to be in four parts: on the way to the park, at the park, the return, and ending. She praised me that mine was good. I wrote:

"The weather was nice then and the teacher took our class for a walk. We went down many streets. On both sides of the streets tower high buildings and in the middle was the traffic. Trolleys are riding on rails, while taxis, wagons and the like don't. There's a swarm of pedestrians about and on the corners policemen.

We played different games in the park, which was all covered with snow. The trees are bare because they have no leaves. Their tops stretch real high. The park has no historical monuments, and only in summer does it have grass. The bushes are covered with juicy leaves.

On the way home we crossed the iron bridge again. We looked at the ice. And we walked back the whole way in pairs.

The trip to the park was very pleasant because it was sunny the whole time and we played different games there."

Compositions are unpleasant because you never write the truth in them. Only, they were assigned.

Mary caught a cold and was ill. And she could have gotten seriously ill and I wouldn't have known. And she could have died because children die too. I seem to be glad that I got the post-card but, in truth, I'm a little disturbed too.

"Why did she come here anyway?"

I only knew a long time ago that I had an aunt in Wilno, maybe I heard even, and that she has some children. Maybe they even said that she had a daughter—Mary. Until I suddenly saw her.

And why? What does it matter to me?

Just a distant relation; some sort of cousin.

If it weren't for my uncle, then I wouldn't even have talked to her. And if she had come to say good-bye, when I was in school, I wouldn't have seen her again.

Maybe I should tear up the post-card and make an end of it?

Why suffer? Why think about it? Why wonder whether she's well, or if something has happened to her?

And I won't answer her anyway, because I don't have any money.

And even if I should get some.

"Here, you rascal," Papa said and gave me a quarter. "Buy yourself what you need, or go to the movies."

But Mama says: "Oh, don't give him any money, you'll only spoil him."

And I took it stupidly and awkwardly. It happened so unexpectedly.

Because Papa was counting up some money: he added up something like thirty one or forty one, and there was a quarter left over. I just happened to be standing there at that moment. And he gave it to me. Unexpectedly.

When I already took it, I felt sorry for Papa. He doesn't have too much and he spends a lot as it is on us children. Instead of buying something for himself, he has to buy for us— a coat, or shoes, food and school and everything. And all he has is a lot of headaches and worries when we misbehave.

When I wanted to be a child, I completely forgot that I won't be earning anything myself, that I'll be a burden.

No. Children aren't free-loaders. School is their job. It's true that we have more vacation time, but the teacher gets a rest too. We work harder than the teacher. Everything is new and difficult for us.

And this is called free-loading—that children don't do anything, that they eat bread for nothing.

When I wanted to be little again, I completely forgot how difficult it is not to have your own money. What slavery it is.

For instance, I have a poor ruler. Someone dented it on me. I left it in good shape and when I came back from recess— it's missing. I looked for it until I found it on another desk. And the edge is all dented. You can't trace evenly with such a ruler— the pencil keeps getting stuck. There are those kind which are edged with steel, but they're expensive. While ours, out of spite, it seems, are made of some soft wood. You forget, you bang it against your desk, and you have a dent right away.

How much damage and loss we suffer. But we say nothing. If you complain to the teacher, she only says: "Be careful." Well, you're not supposed to stay in class during the recess and, anyway can you always be so careful?

Now I have a quarter. That's how it had to be, I guess.

I'll buy Mary a post-card, give back the ten cents to Backiewicz and be finished with Patch. And I'll buy a ruler, to have an extra one. Maybe an extra shoe-lace? Because, if I break one, I won't hear an unpleasant word from Mama. And maybe I'll lend Mundek some money because he may need something.

It would be fun to go to the movies. But how? Should I go alone and then hide the fact from Mundek? And if I tell him that I went, then he'll be hurt.

A quarter seems like a lot. But when you start counting it out, you realize that it's not enough.

And grownups think that children are frivolous. Yes, there are those kind among us, as there are among grownups too. Why does Mundek's father squander money away on drink: There are all sorts. One will steal from his own father, and go and treat others. Or he'll say it's for a pad and spend it on candy. He'll borrow and not pay it back. Or, he'll lose it because he has a hole in his pocket, or it'll fall out with his handkerchief. While another will spend his money only when he has to. He'll save and collect for a long time, penny by penny, for a present for his father or for something which costs a lot.

Mundek and I went to look for a nice post-card. She got an angel while she sent me forget-me-nots. There was one with a boy and girl on it, but I was ashamed, because it looks like it means us.

If you could go into the shop, it would be easier. But it's awkward. They watch you, that you shouldn't take anything, or bend or break something. They're in a hurry too; they don't like it when you look over everything. They'll say:

"Well, hurry up now."

It's clear that they want you to go.

Children only have pennies and so, there's small profit from them.

A grownup doesn't buy all at once either. And they'll let a grownup look through all the albums. No matter that he'll only buy one post-card today; tomorrow, he may spend more.

While we? Pennies and pennies.

I paid back Backiewicz right away. I didn't even have the nerve to ask, until I had some money.

"Here's the ten cents you loaned me."

"I told you I was giving it to you."

"I don't want it. How's Patch doing?"

"How should he be doing?"

He doesn't answer me. Maybe his parents didn't let him keep him; maybe they threw him out.

"Do you have him?"

"And where would he be since you dumped him on me?"

"I didn't dump him, I gave him to you."

"And what if I hadn't taken him?"

"Then maybe somebody else would have."

"And do you think they'll let you bring a dog home just like that?"

I'm getting angry because he's getting so smart.

"Why shouldn't they?" I ask.

"Your parents didn't."

"Because I didn't ask."

I'm angry because it's so easy for him, while I'm still alone. Because a dog's a man's best friend.

I know it's envy—an ugly feeling. But can't you be envious when something goes well for someone else and he doesn't even know how to appreciate it?

I'm curious whether Patch would recognize me. And so, I only swallow my pride and say:

"Could I see him sometime?"

"We-l-l-l, when you come, I'll show you him."

"And could I take him home for a day?"

"Boy! You want everything right away. If he's mine, then he's mine. And maybe you're making a mistake. Maybe he won't want to go with you."

"How do you know? Maybe he would."

"He got used to me already."

"Well, then keep him."

"You bet I will."

I'm walking away. Why should I talk to him? He won't understand anyway.

People seem to talk to one another, but each one feels something else. That's why there's misunderstanding.

There was only Mundek.

We're always together now.

We meet in the morning and go to school together.

And we're together at recess.

He's the only friend I have left now.

But maybe it's wrong to think this way.

Because I have little Irene too, and a mother and father. I also forgot that on the day of parting, we were blowing on a little ball on the table. There was a little ball on the table from something, a watch or something. And Mary said:

"Who can blow the hardest."

And she blew from one side and I from the other.

And we let Irene have a few tries too.

Grey Days

One of the boys lost a second cap already.

There was a big commotion. Mostly in the second grade though. Books and pads disappear there. There was to have been a search. The teachers say that it's a disgrace for the whole school. Everyone reported what he had missing and the teachers noted it down. They didn't take anything of mine. I had a piece of an eraser, maybe a fourth of it. It would have lasted a week yet. I don't know though: maybe I lost it in school; or maybe on the street or at home. And some, when they began to report things, made it sound as if the whole school was full of thieves. Whatever anyone lost or gave away to someone and then forgot about it—everything was reported; the teacher couldn't keep up finally. Some probably lied too. Because Pancewicz is saying:

"Why didn't you tell them that you were missing something? Maybe the school will repay us."

It's even a bigger theft to ask for something to be returned when it wasn't even lost. That kind of a person has no respect for himself.

But there are those kind who really do lose a lot of things. They're not very smart though. That kind will throw something down somewhere and then won't know where. He'll loan something and not remember. And because of them they say that children are careless. Worse yet—they want everyone to be that way. If there's someone who doesn't like to lend things to just anyone, they'll say at once:

"Conceited—miser—stingy."

Often you get real angry, because as soon as he sees something he'll say:

"Let me have it."

Or he threatens you:

"Remember, you'll be sorry! Just you wait, I'll remind you yet. You'll ask me yet."

We have to lend things more than grownups do. They tell you to have things, but if they don't give you them at home, what can you do?

Parents are frequently to blame, while only the child suffers. It's even worse when they don't believe you. Among grownups, when a person's honest, everyone trusts him—but here, the most respectable one of us is suspect.

"I need it for some oak-tag."

"Another one? Why, you just bought one not so long ago."

Such a question hurts. Because, did I eat the piece? A grownup has his own money, and whatever he needs, he buys. But a child gets it only as a favor. He has to wait until his parents are in a good mood, otherwise, they might say something unpleasant.

A child should get a fixed monthly allowance so that he would know just what he has, so that he would learn how to spend, how it make it last. As it is, you either don't have anything, or else, you have too much all at once. This only teaches us how to beg and gamble. He'll be sweet just on purpose, just to get something.

We lose things, forget—that's true. But grownups have big pockets, and desk drawers which no one can go into. And they walk slowly, more deliberately. And even in spite of that they lose and forget things themselves.

When you try, or know, or remember—no one says anything about this; they don't think about how much we try, how much effort we put into things. But just let one thing go wrong and there's a regular scene.

There are cloak-room attendants in theaters. You give them your coat and get a number in return. Then how can something get lost? In school, each one hangs up his own overcoat and then gets it himself afterwards. And on the go yet. And three hundred pupils correctly hang up their coats while only a few throw them any old way. But there's no talk at all about those three hundred orderly ones; only children in general are censured. That's how it looks—wherever there are children it's wrong there, always and everywhere. If it were grownups, it would

144

be different. And when you see that they're offending, that they're humiliating and suspecting, and abusing and punishing, then you either lose all interest in trying, since it seems impossible to satisfy them anyway, or else you do something out of spite.

"Let them yell; what can they do to me?"

You try only to avoid, to retreat, to be as far away as possible, as little with them as possible. Unless, of course, you absolutely have to. Because they're needed when something really hurts you. But if it's only something small—say, if something fell in your eye—it's better if a friend helps you. Otherwise, they jump right on top of you:

"Why this, why that, why, why, why, why...?"

As if I didn't know myself.

Or else, we have to put the blame on someone else. Squealers are rare—and then only in the last extreme. But always with a feeling of fear, that they'll repel you with a bad word, something nasty.

Just think: your own criminals sit behind bars while ours walk freely among us. Yes. We live close to one another—but not together. And just let a child get close, because he likes somebody, and immediately he's suspected of being a "brown-nose," or that he's after something.

And we don't know what's allowed and what we can do; we don't know our own rights and obligations. And this all adds up to disobedience in the eyes of grownups.

I wanted to be little again, to get rid of those grey, adult cares and sorrows, but instead, I have those of a child, and they hurt even more.

Don't let our laughter deceive you.

Look into our thoughts when we're walking quietly to and from school, when we're sitting quietly during a lesson, when we're talking in a whisper or in a quiet voice, or when we're lying in bed at night.

They are different cares and not any the less in degree. But they are felt more strongly—a bigger, greater longing.

You are already hardened to suffering and resignation—we are still rebelling.

When I was a grownup, I was only on guard against a thief. But now it really hurts that they steal.

"Why does one take from another? How can that be?"

It's sad that it can't be good.

"Well, it's too bad," I used to say as a grownup. But now, I really don't want it. I don't want it to be this way.

And I don't believe that school will help. Because grownups seem to be constantly correcting us—and nothing comes of it; they only stir us up even more.

The cap wasn't found. Everyone has to pay for it. And so, you have to tell them about it at home. And at home they'll attack the school at once:

"A school of thieves." Or "What are those teachers doing there; why aren't they watching?"

Again unjustly, because how is the school to blame? The teachers can't watch everything. But the saddest thing is that one person can cause so much unpleasantness and trouble.

Or else, Mundek's waiting for me because I can't find my coat. We both start to search for it.

"What are you two nosing around here for?" the janitor asks straightaway.

"We're not nosing around, only they hung my coat on a different hanger."

"What you didn't hang up, you won't find," the janitor answers back.

"But I didn't come to school without a coat."

"Who knows," he says. And then, a little later: "Well, did you find it? You see: it's there where you hung it."

"You didn't see so you don't know."

"Don't be too smart," he says, "or you'll get it on the ear."

How much time will pass before they not only will stop hitting children, but also will stop threatening them. Because it appears at present that only a few don't hit us, as a kind of favor.

On the way, Mundek again begins to talk about his father.

"You may think that my father's such a drunkard and just creates scenes. In our house there lives such a man. He even brawls. The police had to come once. When he comes home, he beats his wife and children. You hear the blows and then, later, the cries. Afterwards—he'll fall down on the floor—glass or no glass. And then it begins. "It's all mine; I sweated over it; if I want to, I'll smash it, ruin it, burn it up." While his children: "Daddy, Daddy." If it were my father, I don't know what I'd do. Papa only has a weak head; he'll drink a couple of glasses and he's all finished."

146

"But why does he drink?"

"I don't know. He probably got used to it. As for me, I won't drink or smoke. Why drink poison? It even burns your mouth—it'll burn your stomach and blood. I even started to smoke already. But one boy told me to breathe in some smoke and then exhale it through a handkerchief. You should have seen the foul-smelling, yellow stain there was. If I were a king, or had some power, I'd shut all the bars and taverns. If there weren't any, maybe they'd stop drinking."

We walked a little ways in silence.

"There are little balls in the blood into which air enters. The human body's built in a strange way. Not a single machine resembles it. Well, if you don't wind a watch, it stops. But a man goes ten, a hundred years without any winding. I read in the newspaper that someone was even a hundred and forty years old."

And we began to talk about how old some people are. Then about the veterans: that they remember the uprising.

"Would you like to be a veteran?"

"No," he said quickly, "I'd like to be fifteen or twenty years old."

"Then maybe your parents wouldn't be alive anymore," I say.

He thought and thought and sadly says:

"Well, then let it be as it is."

We said good-bye, shook hands, and glanced at one another. While girls always have to kiss, even when they don't happen to like each other very much, we boys are more honest. Or maybe, that's just their custom.

Well, what next?

Nothing, really. All sorts of homework.

In gym, the teacher showed us a new game. There are two sides. You draw a line—that's the boundary. One side is on this side, the other on that one. And each side pulls the other—one person against another, until someone's captured. At first, they interfered because they gave up on purpose, as if they preferred to be with the other side. Or else, they pulled someone over the boundary and he tears away and argues that it's not allowed. But afterwards, it went well. And it was fun.

We asked him to continue to the very end of the hour, to the bell, but the teacher said no. Do I know why though?

As I see it, it would be better to select a few games which everyone likes and let them play them. If there has been touch-tag, sticks, and jostling so many years, and now soccer, why should it be boring all of a sudden? But here, something new at every lesson. That's only irritating, because you never really learn one game well. Well, you may know what it's all about, but you have to play it several weeks to get to know it thoroughly—all the difficulties, all the possibilities, both those that are allowed as well as those that aren't.

To grownups, it seems that children constantly like something new. It's the same with fairy tales. It's true, too that there are those who will start to make faces: "E-e-e-h, we know that already." But if you should ask questions, someone will always start to grimace, that it's uninteresting, that he prefers something else. But we can listen to a nice story, an exciting fairy tale, many times. Grownups themselves will go to the theater to see the same thing, even frequently. Children, on the other hand, rarely go simply to show off—rather, they'd like to know it better.

The game was fun.

Then the superintendent came to arithmetic.

They say that you should try, even if they don't notice you. That we should behave ourselves even when we're not being watched. But they themselves don't always do that.

When the superintendent came, everyone tried harder. Even the principal and the whole school immediately became a model. And it's not clear whom they're afraid of, because the superintendent is kind; he's very pleasant and seems just like any ordinary person.

He told us to calculate the volume of the pen-box. But Drozdowski didn't hear from being so scared and asked: "The lunch-box?"

We thought the superintendent would get angry and then our teacher would be angry at us afterwards. But he's only smiling:

"You're thinking about eating; you must have a great, big appetite," he says.

Everyone began to laugh, but they all answered well. And our teacher told us that it was good. It was a pleasant hour.

And it was the teacher's birthday. It was so cold. We tried to decorate the room with pine boughs. But we didn't have any. And write a greeting for her. But they started to quarrel and nothing came of it. It was to have been a group endeavor; someone was to have written something, and the rest were to have signed their names below it. At first they decided that each one should give five cents. But who would buy the present, and what to write? But nothing came of this. We only drew a few pictures and put them on her desk. While on the blackboard we wrote: "Best Wishes!"

We wanted to add still: "Happiness and Health."

And even: "A handsome husband!"

They were thinking up all sorts of nonsense, but we didn't allow it. And we had to hurry, to finish by the end of recess.

The teacher looked at it and merely smiled. But she must have been touched because there was no lesson, only reading. She brought out a little book, "Our Little One," and read for us for a whole hour.

It was nice—but sad.

Only it's unpleasant when you interrupt the reading and make comments, or explain. Everyone probably understands if he's listening; and even if he doesn't understand, then he'll figure it out later.

But there's always someone to be found who likes to ask questions, while the others are annoyed because he's interrupting. It's rare to find someone who really wants to know. Mostly, that person wants to show off only; he pretends that he doesn't know; he simply wants to appear diligent.

If something isn't very appealing then let them explain and interrupt—time flies faster—but if it's nice, then we're afraid the teacher won't be able to finish it in time. And even if there is something you didn't understand too well, then it ends up sounding even more intriguing.

But she did succeed in reading the whole story and it was only before the bell rang that she thanked the class for the birthday wishes.

I know why. She was afraid at the beginning of the lesson, that they'd start to talk and then, she wouldn't be able to read. Teachers are afraid of every saint in class, every joy, every happy outburst. That's too bad, but it seems that's how it must be.

And we played different games—and that was the whole joy and pleasure of the week. But the sad things—the big and little ones—were numerous. Some were personal, others were a result of feeling sorry for someone else, through sympathy.

Because we, children, suffer a lot when we feel sorry for someone, or when someone's having a hard time.

The teacher tore Hesse's practically new pad. He wrote carelessly in it; well, not so much because he was hurrying, but because his mother is sick and he had a lot to do at home. He didn't even want to do the lesson at all; he was afraid though, that the teacher would get angry. But it turned out even worse. The teacher just happened to be in a bad mood and so, he says:

"Here's a pupil who isn't ashamed to hand the teacher a mess..."

And he tore up the almost new pad.

I don't like Hesse very much. He sits somewhere else and I rarely see him or talk to him. He's wild at play and in joking. He must be very poor too. But I was surprised that he was crying for the first time. Tears were rolling down his face. Then he sat downcast at his desk. I glanced at him once, twice, and went up to him during recess.

When I was a teacher, I was surprised that if someone was justly punished, or maybe hastily, then all the pupils would gather around him immediately and try to cheer him up. Then, even the worst ones will be found among the best, as if they were allies—against me. I'll say: "Don't play with him, don't shake hands with him." While they're against me, and they do just the opposite.

Only now do I understand.

The teacher only accuses while someone else has to defend.

Because it's a known fact that, although a person doesn't say anything, he could, nevertheless, say something in his own defense. Among grownups even the worst criminal has a defender.

He wrote carelessly in his pad. That's strange. Even the laziest person and the one who cares the least, makes some effort in the beginning.

Well?

His mother's sick. If he always happened to write poorly, then now, it's even worse. And then there are even those who can't manage to write nicely at all, though they would like to very much. Either the paper's no good in the cheap pad or else, the nib is old and the blotter smears.

I just happened to have a new pad, and so I gave it to him. He was very happy because now, he says, he won't have to ask his father. It's so difficult at home because of that illness.

He even started something with me a couple of times, but I know now that he won't anymore. We can live at a distance, but in time of trouble you have to help.

Another instance where an act of sympathy was a cause of grief was the following:

The new hygienist found a louse on Kruk's shirt. At once she began to admonish us. Not only him but everyone else—that boy's don't wash themselves, that they have long claws and don't shine their shoes.

(And so, children have claws, while grownups—fingernails.)

Why doesn't she say that one boy has a louse? Why does she have to involve the whole class? And why embarrass the boy to the point where he should cry? Such a thing could happen. And it isn't known where he got it from. We don't always meet with the cleanest ones. We sit together and our coats hang one on top of another. And there's a boarder at home—and he can be dirty. And too, children are always out-of-doors so much.

While here those cuts and insults come immediately. She even dragged our mothers into it. And she had no right at all to do that.

In addition, those teachers' pets, just to ingratiate themselves, have to sound off too: all kinds of biting jibes. And laughter. That repulsive laughter which only hurts and offends.

Shine our shoes? Well, all right: but you have to have a brush and wax and a cloth. What can you do if all the hairs fell out of your brush? And a tiny can of wax costs twenty cents. You can shine your shoes with spittle a few times but after that, even wax won't help.

As if we depend on ourselves.

Worse still is that Mundek has tight shoes. He got a blister and limps even more now. And I have a problem with a large coat while his is even bigger.

He's afraid to say anything at home because they'll start yelling at him: they wanted to buy a pair even one size bigger while even these were already too big.

"I don't know what happened. It must be that a person doesn't always grow at the same rate. That other pair got worn out and was still too big. My foot didn't grow then at all; but

151

now, in the last half year, they've grown so big. I don't know how or when. Everything's tight on me. I can't exercise at all because I'm afraid that everything'll burst—everything's splitting. The teacher's angry that I'm not bending down, that I'm not extending my arms properly, that I'm marching wrong; but he won't take the time or trouble to look and see how I'm dressed."

"What are you going to do?" I ask.

"Do I know... When it gets so bad that I can't walk, then they'll notice it at home themselves. And then, what will be will be. They'll probably yell at me. And maybe even give it to me. It isn't my fault that I'm growing, now, is it? It'll end somehow, this growing."

Then we talked about how they give a little pup whiskey in order to keep it from growing. Maybe that's why there are ponies, because they gave them alcohol. There was such a nice pony last year pulling a circus poster around.

"Did you see him?"

"Of course."

"Where, on New Street?"

"No, on Marshall Avenue."

Grownups are surprised that we quarrel among ourselves even though we appear to be united. Well, that's right, there are two camps: grownups and children. And then, one band against another, and everyone against everyone else. Only Mundek is a true friend—but I don't even know for how long...

My greatest personal worry is that it's not going well for me in school. I'm forgetting what I knew when I was a grownup. Now I can no longer afford not to pay attention during the lesson; I have to listen and do my homework.

It's difficult for me to answer. I'm not sure that I know. And I'm afraid that it won't come out right.

Whenever the teacher looks at the class to call on someone, my heart begins to beat differently then. Maybe it isn't that I'm afraid, but it still isn't too pleasant. It's like an inquest—it's not as if you're guilty, but who knows how it will turn out.

It doesn't depend on me alone, but on the whole class. You answer differently when the whole class knows and understands the lesson and another way when it doesn't. And the teacher is impatient. Just let someone say something silly and it's more difficult to answer correctly after him.

That's why there are days when everybody, even the poorest one, knows, and unlucky days when the whole class seems to have turned into a flock of sheep. Unless, of course, someone doesn't care at all, and starts something on his own. That's when he feels that there are some in the class who are against him, who don't wish him well, and only wait for him to get all mixed up.

It's already hanging in the air, as if they were saying: "Tempt him, tempt him."

Well, it's too bad: I don't know, I don't understand and I can't. Why do I have to understand? Is it really so because I'm not paying attention? Is there no place at all in the world for a less gifted child?

The teacher was calling me to the blackboard. It was to be a correction. But it got all mixed up inside my head. And nothing else but:

"You'll get another zero."

Another person knows how to hem and haw, or puts on a good face or becomes meek and deserving of pity, or else, he knows how to take advantage when they whisper him the answer. It looks like he's working alone, but he's waiting to see what the teacher will say. Or, perhaps, something will happen in the last moment and he'll be rescued?

Everyone helps himself differently, just to twist his way out of a situation. And so do I. But the teacher already remembers me. I don't say that she picks on me deliberately, but she's watching.

They're showing with their fingers that it's time, that the bell's going to ring. But that doesn't help me. Because either she'll keep me after the bell—which is even worse—or she'll not even put a grade down; only she'll remember.

"That's the wrong answer."

I know myself that it's wrong, and I'm only waiting to see whether she'll get angry or whether she'll make fun of me. But it was even worse.

"What's happened to you?" she says with reproach.

"You've become very careless. You don't pay attention during lessons, you write sloppily—you're neglecting yourself completely. And these are the results. Yesterday we were doing a similar problem. Had you paid attention..."

Everything is lost.

Yes, that's right: I went bad. Yes, we go bad and we improve. And never without a reason. Whoever doesn't know what's going on in someone else's head, or what another's feeling inside his heart, he can judge easily.

And so everything was finished.

She doesn't like me any more. And she's annoyed at herself that she made a mistake. It's better to be such a pupil from the very beginning—grey and unnoticed. It's safer, easier—and it's freer. Because they demand less then; you don't have to exert yourself.

I lowered my head and look out from the corners of my eyes because I don't know whether she feels sorry or whether she'll stop liking me.

A teacher will never say if she likes someone. But you can feel it. She has a completely different voice then, a different way of looking at you. Sometimes she spurns you.

You really suffer then, and you can't help it. Or else, you begin to rebel inside. Why am I to blame?

That Baranski thought up a stupid joke and squeezed an orange peel in my eye. It burned a lot but I didn't even make a sound. I only wiped my eyes.

While the teacher: "What are you doing? Instead of paying attention..."

I'm not going to tell, of course. Does it happen only once?

Somebody'll pinch you and you'll scream and jump up. And you're already guilty.

Teachers don't know how we dread those about whom they say: "All quiet on the surface."

He does what he wants and nothing will happen to him. It's unfortunate if you have that kind as your partner at the desk, or if he's behind you. A person is never certain of the time or the hour.

Another time it was even my fault a little.

I'm sitting during the lesson and I notice that Szczawinski has a hand print from chalk on his back. During the recess someone smeared his hand with the eraser and touched him. Szczawinski doesn't know it, but on his back there's a hand imprint.

Well, and I wanted to see whether it was a left hand or a right one. I wanted to measure it even from a distance, but I touched him accidentally. And he turned around. And the teacher yells at him for turning around.

While Wisniewski: "Boy, what paws he's got."

And the teacher questions me. I show him that my hands are clean but he says:

"Both of you stand in the corner."

We didn't stand long. But that's not the point. It's a pity that all our affairs are solved so quickly and just any old way, that for grownups, our lives, our cares and adversities appear to be mere additions to their own real problems.

There seem to be two kinds of life: theirs—serious, worthy of respect, and ours—as if a joke. Because we're smaller and weaker, it's like a game. And this is the source of neglect.

Children—these are future people. And so its a matter of their becoming, it's as if they don't exist yet. But indeed, we are; we live, we feel, we suffer.

Our childhood years—these really are the years of life.

Why? For what reason do they tell us to wait?

Do grownups prepare for old-age? Do they not squander away their strength indifferently? Do they willingly listen to the cautions of grumbling old-timers?

I thought in the greyness of that adult life about the colorful years of childhood. I returned; I let myself be deceived by memories. And thus, I stepped back into the greyness of a child's days and weeks. I didn't gain a thing. Only I lost the armor of indifference.

I'm sad. I feel awful.

I'm ending this strange story.

Events quickly unfold, one after another.

I bring Mary's post-card to school in order to show it to Mundek.

But Wisniewski tore it out of my hand.

"Give it back."

He runs away.

"Give it back, do you hear?"

He's laughing and making his way through the desks.

"Give it back right now."

He waves his hand in the air and shouts:

"Trypshtyck. A letter from his girl friend."

I tear it out of his hand and crumple it and tear it into pieces.

I didn't notice that a piece fell on the ground.

I'm enraged with hurt and anger.

But Wisniewski: "Look, boys. She kisses him a hundred million times."

I run up to him and, bang!—in the face. And then the principal is grabbing me by the hand.

Yes, he's spoiled. And he drew nicely, and wrote well. Now he doesn't pay attention. He's unruly. He does his homework poorly. Call his mother.

"Just you wait. Just let your father come home from work. You won't be getting any more quarters for any movies."

Hemmed in on all sides.

Angry words everywhere, angry glances—forebodings of something even more terrible ahead.

Mundek wants to cheer me up. I know, but I can't. I push him away brutally. I throw the blame on him, thoughtlessly: "It's all because of you."

Mundek's looking at me frightened.

Why? What for?

All because of that post-card.

I hate Mary. She's stupid. A flirt. She'd dance the whole night. She rolls her eyes.

It's too bad it's so far. I'd do something to her from anger. I'd hit her. I'd throw her bow into the gutter.

I'm pulling the plant out of the flower-box...and out the window. Irene has tears in her eyes. She senses that something terrible happened.

It's better not to have anyone, anything.

Where are you, Patch?

No. What do I want with that dog? Let Backiewicz have him with interest. He bought him for ten cents. Let him lick his hand then.

I destroyed all the souvenirs. I finished with the whole world.

I was left alone.

And Mama?

Why, she told me herself that she was renouncing me. That there's only little Irene. Not me. No.

I'm a disgrace and wicked. They all reject me. I'm fed up with life.

Everything is finished. Everywhere deceit.

"He's unruly. He does his homework poorly."

And the teacher, and Patch, and Mama.

I ran all the way up to the very attic and sat down on the stairs in front of the door. It's empty inside me, and all around me.

I'm not thinking of anything anymore.

And I signed from deep inside.

And suddenly a little man appears, clambering through the crack in the door, swaying with a lantern.

"O-o-o-h!"

He's stroking his white beard. He doesn't say anything. He's waiting.

With a hopeless whisper—through tears: "I want to be big again. I long to be a grownup again."

And the little elf's lantern flashed before my eyes.

I'm sitting behind my desk now.

On it there's a huge pile of notebooks to be corrected.

In front of my bed lies a faded rug.

The windows are dusty.

I reach for the first notebook.

There's a mistake on the very first page.

The work 'table' is misspelled. It was written 'tabul.' But

the letter 'u' is crossed out and over it is written an 'e,' while on the very top over the crossed out 'e' appears the letter 'u' again.

I take my marking pencil and in the margin of the paper write: 'tabul,' 'tabul'...

It's too bad. But I don't want to return.

THE CHILD'S RIGHT
TO RESPECT

The Child's Right To Respect

Indifference and Distrust

We learn very early in life that big is more important than little.

—I'm big, a child rejoices upon being lifted up onto a table. I'm taller than you, another affirms with pride, measuring himself against his peer.

It's unpleasant standing on one's tiptoes and not being able to reach or to keep up with a grown-up with one's little steps. A glass easily slips out of a small hand. It's hard for a child to scramble up onto a chair, or into a vehicle, or up a flight of steps; he can't quite grasp the door knob, see out the window, hang something up or take it down because it's too high.

In a crowd the child can't see anything; he isn't noticed or else he's jostled.

It's inconvenient and unpleasant to be little.

It is size and what takes up more space that elicits respect and admiration. Small is equated with ordinary and uninteresting. Little people mean little wants, little joys and sorrows.

A big city, high mountains, a tall tree—these are impressive. We say:

—A big deed, a great person.

A child is small and doesn't weigh much. There's less of him, too. We have to bend down, lower ourselves to him. Even worse—the child is weak.

161

We can lift and toss him up with ease, sit him down against his will, restrain him from running, frustrate his effort.

No matter how often he misbehaves, the adult has a reserve of strength to use against him.

I say:

—Don't go, don't move, move away, give it back.

The child knows that he has to obey. How often does he make an effort unsuccessfully before he understands, gives in and, finally, surrenders.

A feeling of powerlessness summons respect for strength; anyone, and not just an adult, but anyone older and stronger can brutally express dissatisfaction, back up demand with strength and exact obedience: anyone can injure with impunity.

We teach indifference toward the weak by our own example. A bad school is a sign of gloomy things ahead.

The features of the world have changed. It is no longer muscle power that gets the work done or serves as a defense against an enemy. No longer does that power wrest command, bounty and security from land, forests, and seas. The machine has become a subjugated slave. Muscles have lost their exclusive status and value. Knowledge and the intellect have increased in respect.

That heretofore sinister hut, the thinker's cell, has given way to the chambers and laboratories of research. Libraries rise higher and higher, their shelves groaning under the weight of books. The temples of proud reason have become filled with worshipers. The man of reason creates and commands. The hieroglyphs of figures and symbols pour forth new discoveries for the masses; they bear witness to man's power. All this has to be grasped by the mind and understood.

The years of tedious study grow longer and longer—more and more schools, examinations, printed words. While the child is small and weak, has lived but a short time, has not read, does not know...

It's a difficult problem, how to share the conquered places, how to assign tasks and to reward, how to husband the inhabited regions of the globe. What kind and how many factories should be established in order to provide work for hungry hands and brains, how to maintain order and discipline in the human swarm, how to secure protection from an ill will or the madness of a single individual, how to fill the hours of life with activity, rest, and recreation, guard against apathy, satiety, and boredom? How to unite people into a law-abiding community, enhance understanding, when to scatter and divide? Push ahead here, slow down there; here to inflame, there to quell?

Politicians and law-makers make careful attempts. But time and again they err.

And they deliberate and make decisions about the child too; but who asks the child for his opinion and consent; what can he possibly have to say?

Along with reason and knowledge a certain shrewdness helps in the struggle for existence and influence. The one who is alert will pick up the trail and be rewarded handsomely; contrary to reliable judgement, he'll quickly and easily gain his end; he dazzles and awakens envy. It takes cunning to fathom man—no longer the altar but the pigsty of life.

And then there's the child, plodding on clumsily with his schoolbook, ball and doll; he senses that something important and mighty is taking place without his participation, something that spells out fortune and misfortune, something that punishes and rewards. A flower foretells of the future fruit, the chick will become an egg-laying hen, the calf will give milk. In the meantime there is the matter of care, expenses, and worrying: will it survive or not?

The young stir up unrest, anxiety; there is that long period of waiting; maybe he will be a support in old age. But life knows of drought, frosts, and hailstorms which cut down and destroy crops.

We search for signs of the future; we'd like to be able to foretell, to be certain; this anxious anticipation about what the future holds increases our indifference toward what it is.

The market value of the child is small. Only before God and the Law is the apple blossom worth as much as the apple, green shoots as much as a ripe corn-field.

We nurse, shield, feed, and educate. The child gets what he needs without any worrying; what would he be without us to whom he owes everything? Absolutely everything, without exception—only we.

163

We know the way to success; we give directions, advice. We develop virtues, stamp out faults. We guide, correct, train. The child—nothing. We—everything.

We order about and demand obedience.

Morally and legally responsible, knowing and far-seeing, we are the sole judges of the child's actions, movements, thoughts, and plans.

We give instructions and see that they are carried out; thanks to our reason and will—they are our children, our possessions. So, hands off!

(It's true. Things have changed some. It isn't just the exclusive will and authority of the family anymore. There's social control now, however slight, from a distance, barely perceptible.)

A beggar can dispose of his alms at will. The child has nothing of his own and must account for every object freely received for his own use.

He is forbidden to tear, break, or soil; he is forbidden to give anything away as a present; nor is he allowed to refuse anything with a sign of displeasure. The child has to accept things and be satisfied. Everything must be in the right place at the right time according to his regimen.

(Maybe this is the reason why the child values the worthless little things which arouse in adults a surprised compassion: odds and ends, junk—his sole personal wealth—a ball of string, a little box, some beads.)

In return the child is supposed to submit and behave—let him beg, even cheat, as long as he does not demand. Nothing is due him; we give of our own free will. (A painful analogy presents itself: a rich man's mistress). This relationship between adults and children is demoralized by the child's poverty and material dependency.

We treat the child with indifference because he doesn't know anything, doesn't suspect or sense anything.

The child knows nothing of the difficulties and complications of adult life, the sources of our excitement, disappointments, let-downs; what ruins our peace of mind and sours our humor; he knows nothing of adult reverses and losses. It's easy to deceive the child, keep him in the dark. The child imagines that life is simple and straightforward. There's father and mother; father works and earns money and mama shops. He knows nothing about shirking responsibilities nor about how a man goes about struggling for his own well-being and that of others.

Free from material worries, from strong temptations and shocks, the child again does not know and cannot judge. We adults can guess what he's up to at a glance, see through him in an instant. Without having to investigate we detect his clumsy cunning.

Or do we deceive ourselves by judging that the child is no more than what we want him to be? Maybe he conceals himself from us, or suffers in secret?

We level mountains, fell trees, tame animals. Settlements keep on increasing where before there were only swamps and forests. We put people all at once in new lands.

We have subdued the world; metal and beasts have become servants. We have enslaved the coloured races, crudely organized the relationship between nations and tamed the masses. Justice is still a distant thing. There's more hurt and misery.

Childish doubts and apprehensions seem unimportant.

The bright democratism of the child knows no hierarchy. Only fleetingly does he take pity over a laborer's sweaty toil or the hunger pangs of a playmate, the fate of an ill-treated horse, a slaughtered hen. A dog and a bird are close to his heart, a butterfly and flower are his equals; he finds a soul-mate in a stone or a sea-shell. With the haughty pride of an upstart, the child possesses a soul. We do not take the child seriously because he still has a lot of hours of living ahead of him.

We feel the effort of our own steps, the burden of selfish movements, the limitations of our perceptions and sensations. The child runs and jumps, sees things without any apparent motive, is puzzled and asks questions; he sheds tears easily and is profusely happy.

A fine fall day when there's less sunshine is highly valued, as is spring when it's green. It doesn't matter, so little is needed to be happy—effort is unnecessary. Hastily, carelessly we dismiss the child. We treat indifferently the mutliplicity of his life and the joy which is so easily given.

For us precious quarter-hours and years are lost; he has time though, he'll make it, he can wait.

The child is not a soldier; he does not defend his homeland although he suffers together with it.

Since he has no vote, why go to the trouble to gain his good opinion of you. He doesn't threaten, demand, say anything.

Weak, little, poor, dependent—a citizen-to-be only.

Indulgent, rude, brutal—but always indifferent.

The brat. Only a child, a future person, but not yet, not today. He's just going to be.

*

He has to be watched, never to be let out of sight; to be watched and never be left alone; watched at every step.

He may fall, bump himself, get hurt, get dirty, spill, tear, break, misplace, lose, set fire, leave the door open to burglars. He'll hurt himself and us; cripple himself, us, a playmate.

We have to be vigilant, permit no independence of movement, be in full control.

The child does not know how much and what to eat, how much and what to drink, does not know the limits of fatigue. So, you have to supervise his diet, his sleep, his rest.

For how long? As of when? Always. Distrust changes with age; it does not diminish; rather, it even tends to increase.

He does not distinguish the important from the trivial. Order and systematic work are alien to him. He's absent-minded. He'll forget easily, treat lightly, neglect. He doesn't know anything about future responsibilities.

We have to instruct, guide, train, restrain, temper, correct, caution, prevent, impose, and combat.

Combat whim, caprice, and obstinancy.

We have to impose a regimen of caution, foresight, fears and anxieties, presentiments of evil and gloomy forebodings.

We with our experience know how many dangers lie about, obstacles, fatal adventures and calamities.

We know that the greatest precaution doesn't give an absolute guarantee; and this makes us all the more suspicious: in order to have a clear conscience, not to have anything to reproach ourselves for in case of misfortune.

The child delights in the gamble of mischief-making, is curiously drawn to trouble.

He's easily spoiled and hard to correct.

We wish him well, want to make it easy for him; we share all our experience with him without reservation: all he has to do is to reach out—it's all ready for him. We know what is harmful to children; we remember what harmed us. Let him avoid it, be spared; let him not know it.

—Remember, know, understand.

—You will discover, see for yourself.

The child doesn't listen. As if deliberately, out of spite. One has to see to it that he obeys, does what he's supposed to do. Left alone, he avowedly seeks out trouble, chooses the worst path, the most dangerous one.

How can one tolerate senseless mischief, foolish escapades, crazy outbursts?

This to-be is suspect. He appears docile, innocent but, in fact, he's shrewd, cunning.

He manages to slip out from under control, lull vigilance, deceive. He always has an excuse in readiness, an alibi; he conceals or lies outright.

Indifference and distrust, suspicions and accusations. A painful analogy: so he's a trouble-maker, a drunk; he's rebellious, confused. How can one live under the same roof with the likes of him?

Resentment.

It's nothing. We love children. In spite of everything, they are our solace, our delight and hope, our joy and relaxation, the bright sunshine of our life. If we don't frighten, burden, or annoy they feel free and happy...

Why is it though, that there's a sense of a heavy load with them, as if they were an obstruction, an inconvenient addition? Where has this unfavorable opinion toward the beloved child come from?

Even before he greeted the inhospitable world, confusion and limits made their way into the domestic scene. Those brief, irretrievable months of that long-awaited joy seem to break down.

The long period of persistent discomfort ends in illness and pain, sleepless nights and an unexpected expense. Peace at home is disturbed; there is disorder; the budget is thrown out of whack.

To the sharp smell of diapers and the piercing cry of the new-born rattles the chain of marital slavery.

The burden of being unable to communicate, having to imagine, to guess. We wait, even patiently.

When at long last he finally begins to walk and talk—he gets in the way, touches everything, looks into every corner. He is equally obstructive and upsetting, the little sloven, the brat.

He causes damage, opposes our reasonable will. He demands and understands only what satisfies him.

Trifles aren't to be treated lightly: our resentment toward children is cumulative—their waking at wee hours, the crumpled newspaper, a spot on the dress, a smudge on the wallpaper, a wet carpet, broken eyeglasses or a treasured vase and, yes, the doctor's bills.

He doesn't sleep or eat when we'd like him to, when we'd like him not to; here we thought we'd make him laugh and instead he bursts out wailing in fright. And delicate: the slightest neglect and there's the threat of his falling ill, of trouble ahead. If one of the parents forgives, the other blames and nags all the more. In addition to the mother's, there's the opinion formed of the child by the father, the nurse, the maid, the woman next door; against the mother's wishes, and even secretly, each one may mete out punishment.

The little schemer is often the cause of friction and discord among adults; someone is always nasty and getting hurt. For the indulgence of one, the child answers to the other. Often seeming kindness is simply foolish negligence; the responsibility for someone's faults falls on the child.

(Boys and girls don't like to be called children. Sharing that word with the youngest among them burdens the older ones with the responsibility for the past, with the bad reputation of the smaller ones, while, at the same time, suffering the numerous charges hurled at their own group.)

How rarely is the child like we'd like him to be; how often is his growth accompanied by feelings of disappointment.

—By now he ought to ...

The child should reciprocate our good will by trying to repay in kind; he should understand, and give in, control his wants. But above all he should be grateful. Responsibilities and demands increase with age and, as it happens, they are more apt to be different and less than what we should hope for.

A part of the time we relinquish the demands and authority of upbringing to the school. Care is doubled, responsibility increased; divergent authorities collide. Shortcomings begin to surface.

Parents forgive heartily, their indulgence stemming clearly from a feeling of guilt for having given life, for having committed a wrong in the case of a deformed child. It happens that a mother of a supposedly sick child seeks to defend herself against the accusation of others and of her own doubts.

As a rule, the mother's opinion is not to be trusted. It is felt to be biased, incompetent. We rely, rather, on the opinion of teachers, experts, and experienced professionals as to whether the child is deserving of kindness.

A tutor in a private home doesn't often find suitable conditions for coexisting with the children.

Confined by a distrustful discipline, the tutor is forced to vacillate between another's requirements and his own peace and convenience. While bearing the responsibility for the child, he also bears the consequences of dubious decisions of the legitimate guardians—his employers.

Being forced to conceal and to avoid difficulties, he may easily become corrupted by hypocrisy; he becomes disenchanted, apathetic. As the years of work progress, the gap between the adult's demands and the child's desires widens; familiarity with the abject ways of disciplining increases.

Complaints about a thankless job appear; whomever the Almighty wants to punish is called a teacher.

We grow weary of the active, bustling, fascinating life and its mysteries; we tire of questions and expressions of wonder; discoveries and experiments that frequently end with unfortunate results lose their appeal.

Rarely are we advisors and comforters; more frequently we serve as stern judges. A summary sentence and punishment yield the same result: less frequent but, at the same time, stronger and more contrary are the outbursts of boredom and rebellion. As a result, vigilance has to be strengthened, and resistance broken, while measures have to be taken to insure against surprises.

This is the course of the teacher's downfall: he's indifferent, distrustful, and suspicious; he spies on his charges, seizes them unexpectedly, scolds, accuses and punishes them; he looks for opportune ways of prevention; more and more frequently does he impose restrictions, practices tryrannical compulsion; he does not perceive the child's efforts to write neatly a page or simply to live one hour of the day; he declares dryly that it's just hopeless.

Infrequent is that bright blue patch of pardons; more frequent is it the scarlet of anger and indignation.

How much more understanding does educational work with the group require; how much easier is it to fall into the error of accusations and offense.

A single child, small and weak, is wearying. His individual misdeeds enrage. But how annoying, demanding, and limitless in impulse is the behavior of the group.

How difficult it is for a new teacher to take charge of a class or school where the children were kept in the grip of a fierce discipline, where, riotous and alienated, they have organized themselves along the lines of criminal compulsion. How powerful and menacing they are when they oppose your will with collective force, trying to break your grip; they aren't children anymore but a primitive force.

How many aborted revolutions occur about which the teacher says nothing, ashamed to admit that he is weaker than the child.

Once taught a lesson, the teacher will seize upon any means to be able to overcome and prevail. No familiarity, no harmless joking; no mumbling in answering questions, no shrugging of shoulders or gestures of unwillingness; no stubborn silence or angry glances. He will get rid of the problem at the roots, stamp it out vindictively: by indifference and an angry restiveness. He'll buy out the ringleaders with privileges, recruit informers; he doesn't care about just punishment so long as it is severe, to set an example, in order to squelch the first sign of rebellion, so that the group, that force, isn't tempted, not even in thought, to dictate demands or run amok. The child's weakness may evoke tenderness. The power of the group shocks and offends.

There is that false reproach that says that kindness spoils the child and that the response to gentleness is impunity and disorder.

But let's be careful not to label sloppiness, indolence, and silliness as kindness. We find among teachers not only cunning brutes and misanthropes but also rejects from every kind of occupation, persons incapable of maintaining any responsible position.

It happens that the teacher wants to gain the child's favor quickly, easily, and without effort, to worm his way into the child's confidence. He'll choose to banter and joke with the child when he's in good humor, rather than make a real effort to organize community life. At times his lordly indulgence is pierced by sudden outbursts of distemper. He makes himself look ridiculous in the child's eyes.

Sometimes it happens that someone who is ambitious believes that it is easy to reform a person by persuasion and kindly moral teaching, that it suffices to stir and coax a promise of improvement. This is offensive and boring.

It happens that teachers who, on the surface, appear to be friendly with their insincere phrases really turn out to be the child's worst enemies and offenders. These kind arouse aversion.

The response to humiliation will be indifference—to kindness resentment and rebellion, to distrust conspiracy.

Years of work have confirmed for me more and more clearly that children deserve respect, trust, and kindness, that it is pleasant to be with them in a cheerful atmosphere of gentle feelings, merry laughter, an atmosphere of strenuous first efforts and surprises, of pure, clear, and heart-warming joys, that working with children in such an atmosphere is exhilarating, fruitful, and attractive.

One thing, however, has caused me doubt and anxiety: How was it that occasionally the most trustworthy child would let me down? How was it that, though admittedly rarely, there would be a sudden eruption of unruly behavior by a given group? Maybe adults are no better, only more self-controlled, more certain, more reliable and dependable.

Persistently I sought answers to these questions and gradually the following began to dawn on me:

1. If a teacher is intent on seeking out traits and values which seem to him to be especially valuable, if it is his desire to force everyone into a single mold—he will be making a big mistake; some will pretend to follow his tenets while others will genuinely heed his suggestions—for a time. When the real face of the child shows itself, not only the teacher but the child as well will be surely hurt. The greater the effort in pretending to yield to influence—the stormier will be the reaction. Once the child has revealed his real intentions, he has little more to lose. What an important lesson is there in this.

2. The teacher uses one measure of evaluating while the group uses another: both he and the group sense the richness of the spirit; he waits for them to develop, while they wait to see what immediate good will come of those riches, whether he will share what he has, or keep it all to himself as an exclusive privilege—the conceited, jealous, and self-centered miser. He won't tell any stories, won't play games, won't draw or help out, won't be obliging—"he's doing a big favor", "you have to beg him". Alone and isolated, the child makes a strong effort to win the good graces of his own peer community which eagerly accepts his conversion. He did not become spoiled suddenly; on the contrary, he understood perfectly and reformed.

3. I found the following explanation in a book on the training of animals. I don't conceal the source. A lion isn't dangerous when angry, but when playful and eager to frolic; the group is as strong as the lion...

Solutions are to be sought not only in psychology, but even more so in medical books, in sociology, ethnology, history, poetry, criminology, in the prayer book, and in handbooks on animal training. Ars longa.

4. The best but by far not the final explanation dawned on me. A child can become intoxicated with the oxygen of the air as an adult can with alcohol. Excitement, loss of control, recklessness, giddiness; as a reaction, embarrassment, a lump in the throat, a feeling of disgust, and guilt. My own observation is accurate—it is clinical. The most stable person can get tipsy.

Don't scold: this obvious childish intoxication arouses respect and emotion; it does not estrange and set apart, but draws us closer and binds us.

We hide our own faults and guilty actions. Children aren't supposed to criticize; they aren't supposed to notice our bad habits, addictions, and peculiarities. We pose as being perfect. Under the threat of the greatest offense, we defend the secrets of the ruling clan, the caste of the initiated, dedicated to a higher calling. Only the child may be shamelessly degraded and placed in a pillory.

We play with children using marked cards; we pierce the child's weaknesses with the trump cards of adult virtues. As card-sharks we so shuffle the deck as to juxtapose the worst of their hands with the best of ours.

What about our own careless and frivolous grown-ups, selfish gluttons, fools, idlers, rogues, brawlers, cheats, drunkards, and thieves? How about our own violations and crimes—public and private? How much discord, cunning, envy, slander, and blackmail is there among us? Words which wound, deeds which shame? How many quiet family tragedies where children suffer—the first martyrs?

And we dare to blame and accuse?!

To be sure, adult society has been carefully sifted and filtered. How many have been claimed by the grave, by prisons, and insane asylums? How much scum has gone down the gutters?

We urge respect for the elders and the experienced; we caution not to argue with or question them. Children have their own experienced elders among them, close at hand—adolescents with their insistent persuasion and pressure.

Criminal and deranged adults wander about at large; they shove, disrupt, do harm—and they infect. And children on the whole bear joint responsibility for them (because they even give us signals, however faintly, at times). Those few shock public opinion, smudge with conspicuous stains the surface of the child's life. It is they who dictate the routine methods of treatment: keep a tight reign even though it oppresses; be rough even though it hurts, and stern, i.e. brutal.

We do not allow children to organize; disdainful, distrustful, unwilling, we simply do not care. Yet, without the participation of experts we won't be successful. And the expert is the child.

Are we so uncritical as to regard the caresses which we shower upon children as kindness? Don't we understand that on hugging the child it is we who are actually doing the clinging; that we are hiding, helpless, in that child's embrace, seeking in it help and escape in our hours of pain and loneliness? We burden the child with our own sufferings and longings.

Every other kind of endearment which is not an escape into the child or a plea of hope is a crass search for and an awakening of sensuous feelings in him.

—I hug you because I'm sad. Give me a kiss and I'll give you anything you want.

This is egotism, not kindness.

The Right To Respect

There appear to be two lives, one serious and respectable, the other indulgently tolerated, less valuable. We say: a future person, a future worker, a future citizen. That children will be, that they will really begin to be serious only in the future. We kindly let them plod along beside us but, in truth, it would be more convenient without them.

No, not at all. They were and they will be. They did not appear suddenly by surprise, and not just for a brief period either. Children are not a casual encounter who can be passed by hurriedly or dismissed rapidly with a smile and a "Hello".

Children account for a large proportion of mankind, a sizeable portion of the population, of the nation, residents, citizens—constant companions.

Children have been, are, and they will be.

Is there a life that exists as some joke? No, childhood years are long and important ones in the life of man.

A cruel though legitimate law of Greece and Rome allowed for the killing of children. In the Middle Ages fishermen used to catch in their nets the bodies of drowned infants from rivers. In

18th century Paris, older children were sold to beggars, younger ones given away free in front of Notre Dame. Not so very long ago. And to this day they put the screws on children if they happen to get in the way.

The number of illegitimate, abandoned, neglected, exploited, and maltreated children is on the rise. The law protects them, but does it do so sufficiently? Much has changed; old laws need to be revised.

We've grown affluent. We don't get rich solely from the fruits of our own labor. We are heirs to an enormous fortune, share-holders, co-owners. What a lot of cities, buildings, factories, mines, hotels, and theaters we have; what an abundance of goods there is in the markets, how many ships transport them to and fro—the merchants assault the consumers to buy their goods.

Let us tally it all up. Let us calculate how much of the total sum belongs to children, determine the child's share of the profits, not as a favor nor as a charity either. Let us honestly check the amount we allocate for use by the children's portion of the population, how much by the under-age group, and by the working class. What does the inheritance amount to; how should it be divided; have we, dishonest guardians, not disinherited, expropriated?

They are cramped, stifled, poor, and bored.

We have, it's true, introduced universal education, compulsory mental work; we have registration and school taxes. We have also burdened the child with the weight of reconciling the opposing interests of two parallel authorities.

The school makes demands while parents are reluctant to give in. Conflicts between family and school weigh the child down. The parents support charges made against the child that are not always just, defending themselves against the care imposed by the school.

The exertion and effort of an army recruit is also preparation for the day when he might be called up into action; and the state supplies him with all his needs. It supplies him with room and board, a uniform, a weapon, and pay. These are his due; they are not charity.

The child, on the other hand, although subject to compulsory schooling, has to beg from his parents or the authorities.

175

The Geneva law-makers confused duties with rights; the tone of the declaration* is one of persuasion not insistence: an appeal to goodwill, a plea for kindness.

School creates for the child the rhythm of hours, days and years. School officials are supposed to provide for the needs of today's young citizens. The child is a rational being. He knows full well what his needs, difficulties, and obstacles in life are. Needed is not a despotic order, imposed discipline, or distrustful control, but tactful understanding; faith in experience, co-operation and co-existence is the real basis of child-care.

The child is not dumb; there are as many fools among children as there are among adults. Dressed in the clothing of age, how often do we impose thoughtless, uncritical, and impractical regulations. Sometimes a wise child is shocked by a malicious, senile, and abusive ignorance.

The child has a future and a past as well, full of memorable events, memories, and many hours of the most significant solitary reflections. No less than we, he remembers and forgets, appreciates and rejects, reasons logically—and errs when he doesn't know. Thoughtfully he trusts and doubts.

The child is a foreigner who doesn't know the language, isn't familiar with the street plan, is ignorant of the laws and customs of the land. At times he likes to go exploring on his own; when things get rough, he asks for directions and help. What he needs is a guide who will politely answer his questions.

Respect for his lack of knowledge!

A swindler and crook will take advantage of a foreigner's ignorance; he'll give a false answer or mislead deliberately. A boor will mutter something unwillingly. We're always yelling at and quarrelling with children; we nag, reproach, punish. We don't let the child know in a kind way.

How impoverished would be the child's knowledge were it not for his peers, for his eavesdropping; if he didn't pick up information from the words and conversations of adults.

Respect for the effort of learning!

Respect for the setbacks and tears!

---

*Korczak refers here to the Declaration of the Rights of the Child, 1923.

Not only a torn stocking, but a scratched knee; not only a broken glass, but a cut on the finger and a black-and-blue and a bump that's painful.

An ink-blot in his notebook is an accident, an unpleasantness and a misfortune.

—When Daddy spills some tea, Mama says:" It's nothing." But when I do it she gets angry.

Children suffer acutely because they are unaccustomed to pain, wrong-doing, and injustice. More frequently they cry; even a child's tears are treated as a joke, made to seem less important. They make adults angry.

—He whines, bawls, squeals, sobs.

(A chain of words which the adult's dictionary invented for use against children.)

Tears of obstinancy and capriciousness—these are tears of powerlessness and rebellion, a despairing effort of protest, a cry for help, a complaint against indifferent care, evidence that adults restrain unreasonably, coerce, a symptom of a bad frame of mind, but always a sign of suffering.

Respect for the child's belongings and for his budget! The child painfully shares the material worries of the family, feels shortages, compares his own poverty with a friend's affluence. The few pennies that he does possess and that speak of his poverty hurt bitterly. He doesn't want to be a burden.

But what can one do if a new cap is needed, or a movie ticket, or a replacement for a pad or a pencil which was lost or stolen; or if you'd like to buy someone you like a present, or treat yourself to a cake or lend your friend some money? There are so many essential needs, desires, and temptations but no means to satisfy them.

Doesn't it mean anything that in juvenile courts thefts account for the major offense? This is the consequence of treating indifferently the matter of the child's budget, something no amount of punishment will change.

A child's possessions—not junk but a beggar's tools of the trade, hope and mementos. Today's cares and anxieties, the bitterness of the years of youth together with disappointments—these are not illusions but realities.

The child grows. He lives more strenuously. The breathing's faster, the pulse livelier; he's getting bigger—there's more of him all the time; growing deeper into life. He grows day and night, when asleep and awake, happy and sad, when he's afraid, and when he stands cowed before you.

There are spring bursts of double growth and slow-downs of autumn. At one time the bones grow while the heart barely keeps up; at another time there's a slow-down or an excess, a changing chemistry of diminishing and activated glands, a different anxiety and surprise.

At one time he has the urge to run and, like breathing itself, he wants to fight, exert himself, overcome; at another time he feels like hiding, daydreaming, spinning a web of wistful memories. For a change of pace there's a need for peace and quiet, for tenderness and protection. Or else there are strong and passionate desires alternating with fits of depression.

Fatigue, the discomfort of pain, a cold; it's too hot, too cold; drowsiness, hunger, thirst, deprivation, discomfort; or a feeling of having enough—this is not a whim or a school excuse.

Respect for the mysteries and the ups and downs of that difficult task of growing!

Respect for the present moment, for today!

How will he know tomorrow unless we allow him a conscious, responsible life today?

Not to step on, abuse, enslave for tomorrow; not to repress, hurry, drive on.

Respect for every separate moment because each will pass and never return, and always to be treated seriously; injure it and it will bleed, kill it and it will haunt with awful memories.

Let the child drink in the joy of the morning and let him be hopeful. This is how the child wishes it to be. Don't grudge him the time for a story, for a chat with his dog, for catching ball, for the careful study of a picture, or for copying letters. Allow time for this with kindness. The child is really right in this.

Naively we fear death, not realizing that life is but a cycle of dying and reborn moments. A year is but an attempt at understanding eternity for everyday use. A moment lasts as long as a smile or sigh. A mother yearns to bring up her child. She doesn't see this take place because each day it is a different woman who greets the day and bids good night to a different person.

We ineffectively divide the years into more or less mature ones; there is no immature present, no hierarchy of age, no higher or lower grades of pain or joy, hopes or disappointments.

When I play or talk with a child two equally mature moments—mine and the child's—intertwine; when I'm with a group of children, I always say hello or good-bye on the run with a single glance and a smile. When I'm angry, again the feeling is mutual—only that my angry, vindictive moment oppresses and poisons the child's mature and vital moment in life.

Renounce oneself in the name of tomorrow? What attractions are there in this? We paint with excessively dark colors. The prediction is fulfilled: the roof caves in because of a flimsy foundation.

The Child's Right to be Oneself

—What will he be when he grows up?, we ask anxiously.

We want our children to be better than us. We dream about a perfect person of the future.

We have to diligently catch ourselves in lies, pin down our egotism disguised in phony elegance. Seemingly a generous resignation but, in truth, an ordinary swindle.

We have reached an understanding with ourselves, made amends; we have forgiven and freed ourselves from the responsibility of improving. We were badly brought up. It's too late to start now. Our defects and faults have rooted too deeply. We don't let children criticize us, nor do we watch ourselves.

Feeling absolved, we have resigned from the struggle, shifting its burden onto children.

A teacher eagerly adopts the adult's privilege: to keep an eye on the child, not on oneself; to register the child's faults, not one's own.

A child will be blamed for whatever upsets our peace and quiet, our ambition and comfort, for whatever offends and angers us, for whatever runs counter to our own ways, for whatever takes up our time and thought. We don't recognize transgressions without evil intent.

179

The child doesn't know, didn't quite hear or understand, or else misheard, was mislead—it's his fault and ill will.

Not fast enough or a bit too fast, or a task not performed well enough—this is blamed on laziness, sloppiness, absent-mindedness, unwillingness.

Unfulfillment of a harmful, impossible demand—blame. A clumsy, angry suspicion—guilty too. Our anxieties and suspicions are the child's fault as well; he's even blamed for making an extra effort. —You see, if you want to, you can. We always manage to find something to reproach the child for; greedily we demand more.

Do we ever concede to the child tactfully, avoid unnecessary grievances, make living together easier? Aren't we rather the stubborn ones, fussy, offensive, capricious?

The child attracts our attention when he disturbs and causes trouble; we notice and remember only these moments. We take no notice when he's quiet, or thoughtful. We treat lightly those sacred moments of his conversing with himself, the world, and God. The child is forced to conceal his longings and impulses in the face of scorn and brusque attention; he hides his willingness to understand, will not acknowledge his desire to improve.

He dutifully conceals expressions of wonder, anxieties, grievances—and his anger and rebelliousness. We want him to jump and clap his hands, and that's why he shows us the smiling face of a joker.

Bad deeds and bad children make loud noises; they drown out the soft whisper of good. And yet there is a thousand times more good than bad. Good is strong and durable. It's not so that it's easier to spoil than to correct.

We train our attention and ingenuity to prying into wrong-doing, searching, sniffing, stalking, seizing red-handed in the act, full of suspicions of mischief.

(Do we keep old-timers from playing football? How awful is that incessant sniffing about for signs of masturbation in children?)

One banged the door, another didn't make his bed properly, another mislaid his coat, still another ruined his note-book. We scold and nag instead of being glad that these are mishaps that happen only singly.

We hear a lot of complaints and quarrels; but how much more forgiveness there is, giving in, helping, how much more concern and good-will, instruction and positive influence, deep and beautiful.

We want them to be docile, that not a single one of the ten thousand seconds of the school hour (count them) should be troublesome.

Why is one child, for example, seen as bad by one teacher and good by another? We demand uniformity of virtues and moments and, what's more, that children conform to tastes and habits.

Can we find in all of history a similar case of such tyranny? Generations of Negroes have proliferated.

Side by side with health stands illness, alongside virtues and worth there are vices and shortcomings.

For a few children for whom joys and parties are the norm, for whom life is a fable and an inspiring legend full of trust and kindness, there is a mass of children for whom from the earliest days, the world speaks by way of crude words and harsh, sinister truths. They are corrupted by the contemptuous scorn of vulgarity and poverty, or spoiled by the sensual, caressing indifference of surfeit and refinement.

Dirty, distrustful, alienated from people—but not bad.

Not only the home, but the hallway, the corridor, courtyard and street serve the child as models. The child talks in the language of his surroundings, expresses views, imitates gestures, follows examples. There is no such thing as a pure child—every one is tainted to a greater or lesser degree.

Oh, but how quickly does the child free and cleanse himself. There is no medicine for this, just a good wash. And the child willingly helps in this, happy at the chance to rediscover himself. He had been longing for a bath and now he smiles to you and himself.

Such simple victories from stories about orphan children are celebrated by every teacher: these illustrations deceive uncritical moralists into believing that it all comes easily. A fool delights in them, a careerist attributes success to himself, while a tyrant is angry because it isn't the rule; some want to achieve similar results in all areas by increasing the dose of persuasion, others by increasing pressure.

Together with children who are merely sullied, we also meet children who are crippled and injured; there are those kinds of wounds that leave no scars, that heal themselves under a clean dressing. The healing of lacerated wounds however, takes longer; they leave painful scars; they shouldn't be irritated. Sores and ulcers require greater attention and patience.

That folk adage says: "A healing body." One would like to add: "and soul".

How many scratches and contagions are there in schools and nurseries, how many temptations and troublesome whispers; and what a lot of fleeting and innocent activity. We need not have fear of dangerous epidemics where the atmosphere of the school is healthy, where there is plenty of fresh air and sunlight.

How wisely, gradually, and wonderfully does the process of recovery take place! How many wondrous secrets are concealed in the blood, in body secretions and tissues! How every disturbed function and damaged organ strives to regain normalcy, to be back on track! How many marvels are there in the growth of plants and in man, in the heart and brain, in the breathing mechanism! At the faintest emotion or exertion and the heart beats faster, the pulse quickens.

The child's spirit has this same power and endurance. There exist both a moral balance as well as an alertness of the conscience. It isn't true that children are easily infected.

Correctly, though late unfortunately, pedagogy found its way into school programs. Without understanding the harmony of the body, it's impossible to acquire respect for the mysteries of healing.

A botched diagnosis lumps together all kinds of children— the agile, ambitious, critical—all awkward but clean and healthy— with the resentful, sullen, and distrustful—debased, tempted, frivolous, meekly following bad examples. An inexperienced, careless, and shallow observation mixes them all together and equates them erroneously with the fewer criminal and bad types.

(Not only do we adults know how to hurt the orphans of fate but we cleverly benefit from the work of the disinherited.)

Healthy children compelled to mix with such a bad lot suffer doubly: they get hurt and are drawn into delinquency.

While we, do we not accuse indifferently one and all, do we not impose collective responsibility?

—That's what they're like. That's all they can do.

The worst of wrongs.

They are the offspring of drunkenness, rape, and insanity. The misdeeds are but an echo of commands not of an external but an internal voice. A gloomy moment indeed when the child realized that he was different, difficult, a cripple, that he would be ostracized, picked on. The very first decisions are to fight the force dictating bad deeds. What others have gotten so freely and easily, what in others is ordinary and trivial, he receives as the reward of a bloody struggle. He seeks help; if he is trusting, he will come forward, beg and demand: "help me!". He has revealed his secret; he wants to improve, once and for all, all at once, in a single effort.

Instead of thoughtfully slowing down that rash impulse, delaying the decision to improve, we clumsily encourage and urge him on. He wants to free himself while we set a trap for him; he wants to break out while we, in turn, deceitfully prepare a snare. When he expresses a desire to be frank and sincere, we only teach him to conceal.

He offers us a whole day without a flaw, whereas we repel him because of a single bad moment. Is it worth it?

He used to wet his bed every day but now does so less frequently. It was better, then it got worse—no harm. Longer periods between the seizures of an epileptic. The fever of a tubercular has gone down; there's less coughing now. It's not an improvement, but at least it isn't getting any worse. The doctor counts even this as a plus in the treatment. There is no cheating or coercing here.

Desperate, rebellious and contemptuous of the submissive, boot-licking virtues of the mob, these children stand up to the teacher; they have retained one and maybe the last of holies—a loathing of hypocrisy. And this we want to knock down and eliminate. We commit mayhem, resort to the use of starvation and torture to render them powerless; we brutally suppress not rebellion but its open expression. We fan to white heat this loathing toward deceitfulness and cant.

They do not renounce their plan for revenge. Rather, they postpone and wait for an opportune moment. If they believe in good, they will bury their yearning for it in the deepest secrecy.

—Why did you let me be born? Did I ask for such a dog's life?

I reach for the greatest understanding, the most difficult enlightenment. Patient and sympathetic know-how are needed to deal with offenses and misdemeanors; transgressors need love. Their angry rebellion is justified. One has to feel sorry for an easy virtue, measure up to the solitary, damned offense. When, if not now, will he receive the flower of a smile?

In correctional institutions inquisitions are still the rule, medieval penal torture, a united obstinancy and vindictiveness of ill-treatment. Don't you see that the best children feel sorry for the worst: what are they guilty of?

*

Not so long ago the humble physician obediently used to administer sweet elixirs and bitter tonics to the sick; he used to bind the fevered, let blood, and starve his patients in gloomy, funereal waiting rooms. He indulged the powerful and was cold toward the poor.

Finally, he began to make demands—and was granted them.

The physician won space and sunlight for children. Like a general—to our shame—he gave children movement, adventure, the joy of gentle service, the chance on deciding on a decent life, chatting near the camp-fire under a starlit sky.

What is our teacher's role, our area of work? A care-taker of walls and furniture, of order in the playground, of clean ears and floors; a cowherd seeing to it that the herd does not annoy adults in their work and at play; a keeper of torn pants and shoes and a stingy server of meals; a guardian of adult privileges and an indolent performer of unprofessional whims.

What is our teachers' role? A storehouse of admonitions, a dispenser of moral platitudes, and a retailer of denatured knowledge which intimidates, confuses and lulls rather than awakens, animates, and gladdens. Agents of cheap virtues, we have to force from children respect and obedience; we have to stir up sentimental feelings in adults, prod warm emotions from them. To build a solid future on a handful of pennies, to cheat and pretend that children are a number, a will, a force, and a law. The doctor rescued the child from the hands of death; the teacher's job is to let him live, to let him win the right to be a child.

Researchers have affirmed that the adult is guided by motives, the child by impulses, that the adult is logical while the child is caught up in a web of illusory imagination; that the adult has character, a definite moral make-up, while the child is enmeshed in a chaos of instincts and desires. They study the child not as a different psychological being but as a weaker and poorer one. As if adults are everything—all learned professors!

And what about the adult mess, a quagmire of opinions and beliefs, a psychological herd of prejudices and habits, frivolous deeds of fathers and mothers—the whole thing from top to bottom an irresponsible adult life. Negligence, laziness, dull obstinacy, thoughtlessness, adult absurdities, follies, and drinking bouts.

And the seriousness, thoughtfulness, and poise of the child? A child's solid commitment and experience; a treasure chest of fair judgements and appraisals, a tactful restraint of demands, full of subtle feelings and an unerring sense of right.

Does everyone win playing chess with a child?

Let us demand respect for those clear eyes and smooth temples, that young effort and trust. Why is it that we show respect for that spiritless expression, that wrinkled brow, bristled greyness, stooped resignation?

There is a sunrise and a sunset, a morning as well as an evening prayer; every inhalation has an exhalation; for every systole there is a diastole.

A soldier, when he moves out to battle and returns, is covered with grime. A new generation is mounting, a new wave is gathering. They come with vices and assets; give them conditions under which they can develop better. We won't win a case against the coffin of a sick childhood; we can't order a cornflower to be wheat.

We aren't miracle-workers—nor do we want to be charlatans. Let us renounce the deceptive longing for perfect children.

We demand that hunger be eliminated, cold, dampness, overcrowding, overpopulation.

It is you who bear the sick and the crippled; it is you who create conditions for rebellion and contagion: your thoughtlessness, ignorance, and lack of order.

Beware: contemporary life is shaping a powerful brute, a homo rapax; it is he who dictates the mode of living. His concessions to the weak are a lie, his respect for the aged, for women's rights and kindness toward children are falsehoods. Such homeless sentiments wander about lost, like Cinderella. Rather, it is really children who are the real princes of feelings, the poets and thinkers.

Respect, if not humility, toward the white, bright, and unquenchable holy childhood.